D1757043

Planetary Gardens – The Landscape Architecture of Gilles Clément

Alessandro Rocca (Ed.)

Planetary Gardens

The Landscape Architecture of Gilles Clément

Birkhäuser

Basel · Boston · Berlin

© 2007 of the original edition: 22publishing, Milan
The Italian edition of this book was published under the title
"Gilles Clément. Nove giardini planetari"
22publishing S.r.l.
via Morozzo della Rocca 9
20123 Milan, Italy
www.22publishing.it

Translation into English:
transiting_s.piccolo

Book design: Giovanni C. Russo & Fabio Luis Soletti / No 11, Inc.
Editorial staff: Maria Francesca Tatarella
Layout and cover design of the English edition: Alexandra Zöller

Library of Congress Control Number: 2008929297

Bibliographic information published by the Deutsche Nationalbibliothek
The Deutsche Nationalbibliothek lists this publication in the Deutsche
Nationalbibliografie; detailed bibliographic data are available on the Internet at
http://dnb.d-nb.de.

© 2008 of the English edition:
Birkhäuser Verlag AG
Basel · Boston · Berlin
P.O. Box 133, CH-4010 Basel, Switzerland
Part of Springer Science+Business Media

Printed on acid-free paper produced from chlorine-free pulp. TCF ∞

Printed in Italy by Geca Spa

ISBN: 978-3-7643-8781-5

9 8 7 6 5 4 3 2 1

www.birkhauser.ch

I.

II.

III.

THE NOMADIC GARDEN, THE PERMANENT TRAVELLER

BY ALESSANDRO ROCCA

GILLES C
GUIDELIN
THE PLAN
GARDEN

LEMENT

NES FOR

NETARY

THE NOMADIC GARDEN,
THE PERMANENT TRAVELLER

The projects and ideas of Gilles Clément form a fundamental point of reference today for anyone interested in landscape and its related themes. His work has something to tell us all – urban planners and gardeners, politicians and administrators, architects, ecologists, farmers and landscape enthusiasts – because it addresses the deeper issues, the crucial themes of nature, environment and landscape, stimulating reflection and comparisons. His interventions do not offer beautiful, facile solutions, but a way of thinking that challenges habits and clichés, introducing an incredible quantity of energy, freedom and creativity in our relationship with nature. Radical, courageous, holistic, the thinking of GC is never elitist, never prone to intellectualism. His concepts are clear and powerful, the images of his gardens strange and seductive. His message is loud and clear, easily accessible for all who are willing to listen. Their ranks are growing in number and interest, because his reasoning is directly rooted in two of the foremost themes of our time: ecology and globalism. In the commitment of GC these two terms merge to produce fragments of nature, gardens, that demonstrate the possibility of making a better world: more beautiful, healthier, more interesting.

The extraordinary work of GC defies the rules and formulae usually applied by successful landscape designers. For example, it is lacking in any signs that can act as trademarks, and it eschews the simplifications that seem inevitable to make inroads in mass media and public opinion. GC does without the stigmata of success, the public fraternizing of VIPs and the presence of politicians, and carefully avoids all status symbols. He is an independent spirit, who over the course of more than forty years – he sets Spring 1968 as the symbolic beginning of his intellectual adventure, when suspension of classes gave him a chance to conduct research in the field, for the first time – has constructed a solid, complex theory, reinforced by a series of very convincing practical demonstrations.

The originality of his œuvre, his projects and his many writings has made him immune, at least until now, to any credible attempts at imitation, but this does not mean that stimulating parallels have not emerged between his work and that of other landscape designers. One important reference, for example, has been Michel Corajoud, doyen of contemporary landscape architecture in France, and significant correspondences connect him with other very interesting landscape talents like Michel Desvigne and Catherine Mosbach, or the Dutch gardener Piet Oudolf. So his path has been essentially solitary, though taken in the midst of many admirers and supporters, and with the not infrequent company of some of them, along certain stretches of the way:

THE GARDEN IN MOVEMENT

"The Garden in Movement interprets and develops the energies found in the place, and attempts to work as much as possible with, and as little as possible against, nature. Its name refers to the physical movement of plant species on the land, which the gardener interprets in his own way. Flowers grown in the middle of a path oblige the gardener to choose: should he conserve the passage or the flowers? The Garden in Movement recommends respect for the species that settle there in an autonomous way. These principles disrupt the formal conception of the garden that, in this case, is totally entrusted to the hands of the gardener. The design of the garden, which constantly changes, is the result of the work of the person who maintains it, not of an idea developed at the drawing board."

the nomadic garden, the permanent traveller

1. Gilles Clément, *Les Jardins du Rayol*, Actes Sud / Dexia éditions, 1999.

2. Alain Roger, *Dal giardino in movimento al giardino planetario*, in "Lotus Navigator" n. 02, 2001.

an experience, a project, a line of reasoning. His work fascinates all those who prefer process to form, discussion to dogma, experimentation to the celebration of certainties. Architects sharing a similar design approach find his ideas very intriguing; agronomists find suggestions on how to interpret everyday problems of great ideological and practical impact, such as questions on the presumable authenticity and appropriateness of native vegetation. But GC's message also has significant repercussions in the political debate, introducing a series of arguments that clearly urge us toward a more balanced world, but also one that is more open (and open to change). His supporters follow closely his movements along routes that belong – as in any true journey – only to those who take them. And in his case the journey is not just a metaphor, because for GC travel has always represented, ever since his first long stay in Nicaragua, an opportunity for study and reflections. Over the years, his study of nature has focused, above all, on the identification and analysis of climates and environments comparable to those of the Mediterranean zone: California, Chile, certain regions of China and Australia, New Zealand.

The most complete, effective application of these investigations takes place in the Domaine du Rayol, the garden on the coast of Provence, organized as a collage of "Mediterranean" fragments from five continents[1]. In other ways, GC's travel represents a recognition of nomadism as a way of living, a practice that thrives on research, a taste for discovery, the awareness that everything we may encounter has to do with us, directly: we are all nomads and all natives of the same place, the same planet. The first effect of nomadism – of men, but also of animals and plants – is that "every garden (in movement or not) is a planetary index". As Alain Roger reminds us, one of Clément's favourite examples, and also the most instructive, is that of the untended areas of Paris (untamed, unlike the Garden in Movement), which far from being truly native, as one might imagine, 'are composed above all of American locusts, Asian buddleia and ailanthus, and even a small Siberian artemisia that carpets bare soil'. In short, a biological mixture as an index with an exceptional value"[2].

THE GARDEN IN MOVEMENT 2

"Instructions for use: take a piece of land suited to your resources, wait for the September rains and then sow a mixture of different seeds you have prepared. Plunge your hands into the oilseed flax and phacelia pods and make the sweeping gesture of the sower, pushing your arms forward and letting the seeds sift through your fingers. Start again, following the rhythm of your steps, until you have sown all the seeds. Wait two or three weeks and then return there, one morning, to observe the seedlings of corn cockles, poppies, hound's-tongue, borage, mullein and bluebottles, forming a green and grey fuzz on the ground. Do nothing until the following spring. Make the islands and, between them, the path, and repeat the trimming along the same paths, until July. In this period the garden is blooming with species that rapidly vanish, and in September there will be another period of flowering, of different species. Remove the islands of wilted flowers as soon as their seeds have been scattered. Take care not to uproot the new seedlings and make other islands. The paths form by themselves and even the most recent ones have already changed their route. Return to the garden and you will see that everything is different and everything is the same, all full of mushroom volutes and other surprises: you are about to invent the Garden in Movement!"

the nomadic garden, the permanent traveller

3. Gilles Clément, *Le jardin en mouvement*, Sens et Tonka, 1994.

4. Gilles Clément, *Le jardin planétaire. Réconcilier l'homme et la nature*, Albin Michel, 1999, catalogue of the exhibition *Le jardin planétaire*, Grande Halle de la Villette, Paris, 1999-2000.

5. Gilles Deleuze, Félix Guattari, *Mille plateaux*, Éditions de Minuit, 1980.

The Garden in Movement [3] and the Planetary Garden [4], the two concepts that form the basis for GC's vision and design, call for and support a nomadic conception of man and nature. Movement, wanderlust, migration and mixture are the operative agents of an uncertain system in which chance plays a leading role in the creation of constantly changing arrangements.

THE PROJECT AS AN UNCERTAIN SYSTEM

GC is a naturalist who studies life, its biological and social aspects. But he is also a humanist who has managed to transfer the complexity, uncertainty and extraordinary variability of factors belonging closely to the random structure of life itself into design action. He has taken on the status of a permanent traveller. In fact, his Planetary Garden is based on two paradoxically contradictory convictions. The first implies the end of travel, in the sense that wherever we go we always remain here, on the Earth, in our garden; the second indicates the identity between life and voyage, already interpreted by the Garden in Movement, that tends to change location, to migrate, to be born and to die, like an equivalent of life itself. These two hypotheses (which like asymptotic curves never come to meet in their perspectives) are the sources of a vagabond (or "nomad", according to Gilles Deleuze and Félix Guattari) science, that traces the mobile coordinates of a destabilized design field, divested of the responsibility

of beauty and charged with the necessity of a true, dynamic, critical relationship with the natural environment. GC's movement does not follow an itinerary, does not take aim at a destination. It is nomadic and, at the same time, chaotic, since it remains inside a pre-set perimeter (the garden) that borders a space of freedom in which to follow unpredictable, recurring yet extemporaneous routes. As Deleuze and Guattari describe it, in *Mille plateaux* [5], "the nomadic route may well follow the usual tracks or roads, but it does not have the function, as in the routes of the settled world, of distributing a closed space to men, assigning each one his part and regulating the communication among the parts. The nomadic route does the opposite, it distributes men (or animals) in an open, indefinite space … this is a very particular distribution, without division, in a space without boundaries and without closure". The Garden in Movement is a laboratory of permanent nomadism, an always active centre of reception, a place of encounters and disappearances, of the aleatory or, at best, of seasonal certainties. In a certain sense, the Garden in Movement – and this is another paradoxical aspect – belongs to the Non-Places, those sites described by Marc Augé that lack history, permanence and identity. With respect to vital flux – of men, plants and animals – the Garden in Movement is like a way station, a routing hub, a logistics park of nature in which energies converge and are redistributed, energies that would not be welcome in other contexts, such as those of traditional gardens or cultivated lands.

THE GARDEN IN MOVEMENT 3

"Plants travel. Especially the herbs.

They move in silence, like the wind. Nothing can be done about the wind.

Were we to harvest the clouds, we would be surprised to find unpredictable seeds mixed with loess, fertile silt. Unthinkable landscapes are already being designed in the sky.

Evolution has its advantages, but not society. The most modest management project runs up against the calendar of programming: to put in order, to rank, to tax, when everything can change in an instant. How can we maintain the landscape, what technocratic grid can we apply to the intemperance of nature, its violence? The project of total control finds unexpected allies: the radicals of ecology and those of nostalgia. Nothing must change, our past is at stake; or, nothing must change, biodiversity is at stake. Everyone against nomadism!"

the nomadic garden, the permanent traveller

THE PHILOSOPHER IN THE GARDEN

The charm and the difficulty of GC's work come from the overwhelming presence of statements, themes and models that would suffice to sustain the work of at least ten individual designers. Though every concept is defined and developed clearly, with great literary and graphic pertinence, the range of the technical background and the philosophical scope of the discussion are bewilderingly vast. In an attempt at orientation we start looking for contradictions, for the missing link that might reduce the theoretical construct to a refined exercise in design creativity. But the quantity of the available material – books, interviews and projects – is immense and too well-structured to be reduced to a compendium of suggestions and recipes, ready to be used.

The evocative power acts as an attraction, an invitation to grasp a vision of the world that focuses on the universe of living things and their garden, planet Earth. The importance of the subject makes the thinking, at times, radiate almost religious overtones, appearing as a secular, rational, profoundly humanistic creed that opposes the technical dominion with an alternative, very seductive path – a complex, clear and elegant theory, supported by a series of realisations. Fortunately it is a religion that is not based on dogma, but on reasoning, open to change, ready to run the risk of confrontation with other currents of contemporary thought, taking part every day in the debate on the various moral and political options involved. This is factive, operative thought, with educational clarity and a strong demonstrative character. GC wants to persuade and to convince, aware of how hard it is to get beyond the barriers of habit and the most reassuring clichés. The stated objective, pursued with great success in the exhibition on *Le jardin planétaire* (Grande Halle de la Villette, Paris, 1999-2000), is the development and spread of a new approach based on close, informal, productive interaction with nature.

It is also elastic, democratic, flexible thinking. In tune with the most interesting dynamics of today's design culture, the cardinal concepts of the garden of GC are change, multiplicity, randomness and holistic unity. To paraphrase his three guiding concepts, we might say that his theory combines "thought in movement", "planetary thought" and "third thought" in a way of reasoning that is absolutely original and personal, but already organized to be transformed into shared knowledge, to become a catalyst of political action (GC is no stranger to such commitment, as demonstrated by his impassioned public statements following the election of Nicolas Sarkozy as

UNTILLED LAND

"I love untilled land, because there is nothing there that has to do with death. A walk in an untended place is open to all questions, because everything that happens there is bound to elude even the most adventurous speculations. The fact that the IFLA (International Federation of Landscape Architects) classifies abandoned industrial areas as endangered landscapes is a truly revealing signal. The reappropriation of land by nature is interpreted as decay, when it is actually the exact opposite. This is a leftover stereotype, like the idea that man should never relinquish the land he has tamed. Everything man relinquishes to time gives the landscape a chance to be simultaneously marked by his presence and freed from it."

6. His appeal was published, as soon as the election results were known, at the website www.gillesclement.com.

French President[6]). This wide gaze takes in local situations and connects them on a planetary scale, in a passage that develops great operative power in terms of both communication and design. GC's thinking eliminates the irresolvable unknown, the mystical, eschatological component, linking man and nature in a single destiny. Transforming the planet into a garden makes it impossible to avoid individual or collective responsibilities. Living nature is no longer an abstract concept but a real place, planet Earth, and it is also each of its individual parts, every plant, every animal, every man. An interconnected system, exceptionally complex but finite, measurable, explorable: a gigantic Garden in Movement whose most precious value is the possibility of continuing change, in an evolutionary process that is apparently random and endless.

The whole system of the natural world, according to the ideal diagram drawn by GC, is a garden, and as such it is a circumscribed space that can be controlled: a project.

Therefore the idea of the Planetary Garden is extremely effective, because it represents the degree of unity and interdependence of the elements, and our direct responsibility in the management, or the destruction, of the entire living system. The planetary conception is based, above all, on the holistic, communitarian and totalizing aspect, but the idea of the garden contains another concept, that of the project, the design. If we refrain from applying the usual aesthetic criteria to the Planetary Garden, we can see that the backbone of GC's reasoning is the hypothesis that the world is the result of a design action that can never stop and coincides, in the end, with life itself.

BEAUTIFUL?

"Nothing is more damaging for our profession than the sense of inferiority a landscape designer feels with respect to architects, leading him to attempt, without success, to get closer to a profession he will never practice, while failing to continue with deeper

THE PLANETARY GARDEN

"Every fragment of space shaped by man can be seen as a palimpsest on which to etch and overlay grand visions of the world. We need to encourage a higher awareness, determined by the interaction of living beings, but also of their cultural systems: a simultaneously plural and unitary eco-ethnological system. A great garden, a small planet. The Planetary Garden comes from the combination between nomadic observation and a hypothesis: can we see the earth as a single garden? And can we apply the precepts of the Garden in Movement to it? The Planetary Garden is a principle, and its gardener is all of humankind."

the nomadic garden, the permanent traveller

7. Gilles Clément, *Où en est l'herbe? Réflexions sur le jardin planétaire*, Actes Sud, 2006.

study of all the increasingly rich, profound things that make him closer to gardeners. Knowledge of the slow, demanding living world discourages the lovers of the surface, the artists of prêt-à-porter, the architects of smooth, sharp, reflecting materials, those who see reality as a purely, simply formal system"[7].

Will the Garden in Movement be beautiful or ugly? Or should we ask, instead, if it will be right or wrong? In my view both questions represent false problems, rhetorical queries destined to remain unanswered. The central issue lies elsewhere; the Garden in Movement, as materialized in La Vallée and other projects (Domaine du Rayol, Parc Citroën, Parc Matisse), is a representation that extends in space and time, a ceremonial happening in which the timing and modes of any intervention can be dictated only by the person responsible for the liturgy, the philosopher-gardener. The haruspice reads, interprets and decides what action to take, in keeping with a strategy that, beyond any reasoning, retains a strong arbitrary component. The second identity of the philosopher-gardener is found in this decision-making sphere, and is expressed not through concepts but through form, the perception and organization of space. At this point, with the traditional approach of design pushed into the background, the project develops through a botanical choreography that follows impulses and techniques. They have nothing random about them, and may appear to the visitor as a rebus that is not easy to solve. In these gardens nature expresses a strong, disturbing, rather enigmatic spectacle. At the same time, the absence of traditional design brings these gardens closer to a type of nature to which we are no longer accustomed: landscape as developed for economic and productive rather than aesthetic ends: the

THE THIRD LANDSCAPE

"The whole of abandoned spaces, which are the main territories of refuge for biological diversity. It includes leftover territory, both rural and urban, and the untilled zones: the edges of roads and fields, of industrial areas and nature reserves. It is the space of indecision, and the living things that occupy it act freely. To see the Third Landscape as a biological necessity that influences the future of living things modifies our interpretation of the territory, attributing value to places that are normally neglected."

the nomadic garden, the permanent traveller

rural landscape of the past, rich in different species but also in uncultivated corners, not yet transformed into the agricultural desert of industrial production, weed killers and intensive monocultures. The landscape still found in the Third World or in those leftover parts of the urbanized territory that have been preserved, usually through chance or neglect from contact with man, like the weeds growing between railroad tracks, the meadows in the midst of a highway cloverleaf, the plaza of an abandoned industrial complex: fragments of the Third Landscape.

The gardens of GC glow with the magical aura that illuminates those rare successful unions of concept and matter, they glow with that sense of secret complicity found at archaeological sites, where the tracks of human activity, faded by the passage of time, are diluted and mingle with the host environment. This is the same poetry that awaits us in abandoned places of spontaneous growth, a piece of the Amazon jungle or a neglected expanse of asphalt, ready for the invasion of pioneer species. Another borderline was crossed with the creation, in a public park, of an ecological island for total preservation. The island of Derborence, in the Parc Matisse at Euralille, is a platform elevated seven meters above the level of the park, made by collecting the debris from the construction of a railway. With some initial prompting, the small plateau has been colonized by pioneer species, giving rise to a process of naturalization that truly starts from zero. In this sense this island is an alternative, natural, pacifist Ground Zero, a place of re-beginning, where man cannot set foot. Only the chief gardener of the park makes an inspection, each year, analyzing the growth of the island and collecting information on this singular ecological experiment.

ENDEMISM AND DIVERSITY

"Endemism is diversity caused by isolation, diversity of living beings and ideas. Geographical isolation and climate barriers create settings in which species appear.

The more places of life, or biotopes, there are, the more species will be capable of living in them, the more societies will develop in them.

The greater the period of isolation between biotopes, the greater the diversity that can dwell in them. Diversity is expressed in the variety of individuals, behaviours, beliefs."

the nomadic garden, the permanent traveller

8. Gilles Clément, *La sagesse du jardinier*, L'oeuil neuf éditions, 2004, p. 43.

9. Gilles Clément, Louisa Jones, *Gilles Clément. Une écologie humaniste*, Aubanel, 2006, pp. 74-75.

NON-VIOLENT LANDSCAPING

The philosophy, writing and projects of GC are marked by a deep aversion for any form of violence. Violence seems like a threshold never crossed, a veritable taboo that forms a contrast with the radical spirit of all the thinking and work of GC. The calm tone and painstaking attention to the natural world, similar to the approach of a scientist, should not overshadow (though they often do) the ideological depth and subversive impact of the proposal. GC's approach implies profound rethinking of traditional design: citations and remnants of classical composition appear, unexpectedly, as decontextualized fragments, or as models emptied of meaning by now, but still subject to recovery, inhabitable abodes for ideas that have little to do with the legacy of the past. "The art of gardens has expressed excellence by way of architecture and ornament, dimensions that are no longer sufficient today. The life that grows in the garden, since it is threatened, becomes the main argument of the project. And the force of this resolve overrides, without prohibiting them, the notions of the past: ordering the perspective, arranging landscapes in views, quelling the masses, organizing celebrations and distractions, etc. At this point we must work on what is alive: to consider it, to know about it. And befriend it"[8]. Furthermore: "The natural garden becomes the biological garden, domination becomes association, spectacle gives way to participation, observation of vital processes takes the place of manipulation, what was static becomes dynamic"[9].

In his most didactic, reflective text, published in the book *La sagesse du jardinier*, GC engagingly narrates childhood memories and early experiences with gardening, conducted under the guidance of his father. The main theme of his reflections is the contrast between the spontaneous movement of nature and the constraining rules imposed by the aesthetic ideal of the gardener. The most significant and most entertaining episode has to do with moles, a true scourge of grassy lawns. Strychnine, smoke, broken glass, ambushes and other persecutions failed to achieve the goal of total extermination. As a final remedy the gardener (Clément the elder) shot at the poor animals with a rifle; even when he missed, they died anyway, felled by the shock of the sudden explosion.

This experience is narrated by GC as an example of authoritarian, near-sighted, wasteful gardening that applies great amounts of energy to battle, repress and destroy the "disastrous" creativity of the natural world. He believes in quite the opposite approach, and all his projects can be interpreted as steps in a progressive rapprochement with nature, in research that experiments with different means and modes to develop a new ideal and practical coexistence between man and the natural elements of the environment.

Thus the relationship with the traditional and even the modern way of designing the garden is interpreted in terms of evolution, as a passage to a more advanced phase. It is a soft process, but only apparently so. Its selective approach is not limited to liquidation of an important heritage that, in any case, has already been entirely used up. It also actively takes on another contemporary hypothesis, the landscape design that would update the art of the garden based on static composition, utilizing as its main references not botany and ecology, but the world of figuration, of more or less artistic origin.

For GC (who in this and other aspects is close to other branches of contemporary art)

MINGLING AND DIVERSITY

"Mingling threatens diversity and, at the same time, produces new situations and new living beings. Speeding up the pace of his movements on the earth, man, consciously or not, speeds up the mingling of species, nourishing the untended. It is necessary, in fact, to have the combination of two factors: the seeds and a host surface. Mingling is at work in every corner of the planet. Certain ubiquitous species are considered cosmopolitan, by now: ferns, mullein, eucalyptus, mimosa. Planetary mixing touches all living beings and, above all, those equipped with a wider biological spectrum. Sapiens, the only species of the Homo genus, has an immense spectrum and mixes its natural varieties – the so-called races – with energy and difficulty. The result is a chromatic *métissage* accompanied by the singular characteristics that unite, amidst differences, the human species. All humans are capable of interbreeding with other humans and producing fertile offspring. This is the definition of a species. So it is natural, or even desirable, for mingling to take place."

the nomadic garden, the permanent traveller

10. Gilles Clément, Louisa Jones, op. cit., p. 73.

11. Gilles Clément, Louisa Jones, op. cit., p. 18.

12. Gilles Clément, Louisa Jones, op. cit., p. 38.

what counts most, the first and last reference point of any project, is not the design or even the concept, but life: "The idea is not to create the illusion of nature, as in the Romantic garden, but to take part in a vital flux that is already present and active in that place"[10]. In other words, it is life that nourishes, animates and transforms the garden. The first, very effective slogan that captures the thought of GC is "the Garden in Movement, the space of life left free for development of the species that establish themselves there"[11]. A garden freed from what? From the tyranny of beauty, the aesthetic paradigm. As he already said in 1989, "a generation of landscape designers has used a language of architects. I have conceived gardens away from

any aesthetic considerations, because decor is filler, like any other. Gradually two things have emerged, signification and biology, in the widest sense of the term: movement, energy"[12].

The gardener is a facilitator of life, someone who "does the most he can with, and the least possible against (nature)". His task is to "maintain and increase the biological quality of the substrates: earth, water, air, and to intervene with the greatest economy of means, in order to limit tangles, accumulations of water, the passage of cars."

The non-violent strategy of GC subjects the garden – perhaps one of the environments most resistant to the changes of modernity – to a total revision. The Garden in

THE THEORETICAL CONTINENT

"Assembled in a single figure, the whole set of the biomes (the major climate sectors of the planet) reflects a present biological reality, the result of the planetary mingling of living beings. With the exception of certain species with a particularly wide biological spectrum, plants and animals never surpass the limits of their biome. Man, on the other hand, can live in all the climate sectors of the world."

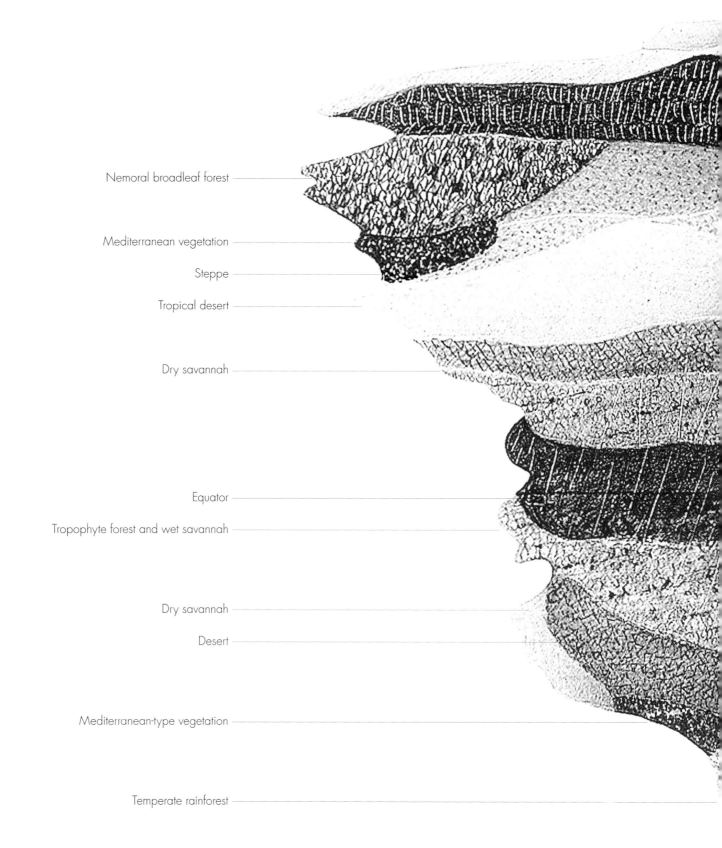

Nemoral broadleaf forest

Mediterranean vegetation

Steppe

Tropical desert

Dry savannah

Equator

Tropophyte forest and wet savannah

Dry savannah

Desert

Mediterranean-type vegetation

Temperate rainforest

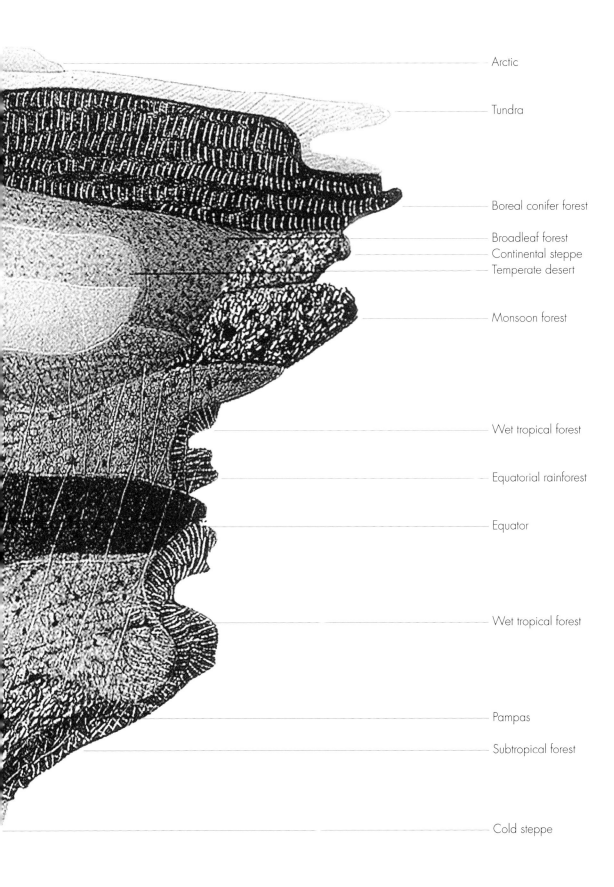

Arctic

Tundra

Boreal conifer forest

Broadleaf forest
Continental steppe
Temperate desert

Monsoon forest

Wet tropical forest

Equatorial rainforest

Equator

Wet tropical forest

Pampas

Subtropical forest

Cold steppe

The theoretical continent. Drawing by Gilles Clément that groups the major climate areas with their vegetation (from Troll and Ozenda, 1968).

the nomadic garden, the permanent traveller

Movement is democratic and anarchic, a chaotic system whose definitive arrangement is one of permanent revolution.

THE MANIFESTO LANDSCAPE

The most complete (and perhaps the most seductive) expression of the radicalism of GC is found in the concept of the Third Landscape[13], a term borrowed from the idea of the "Third Estate" (not the Third World, though the connection is certainly not coincidental). Abbé Sieyès, uttering a phrase that would enter the annals of French history (of the Revolution), put it as follows: "What is the Third Estate? Everything. What has it been hitherto? Nothing. What does it desire to become? Something."

The Third Landscape, according to GC, "is the extension of the two concepts I have formulated in my work over the last thirty years. The Garden in Movement, the result of the experience of my own gardens in La Creuse (La Vallée and Le Champ), and the Planetary Garden, a project that involves a more political dimension. It examines the coherent system that forms the relationship between man and environment, and was developed in the exhibition of the same name at the Grande Halle de la Villette in Paris at the end of 1999. *The Manifesto of the Third Landscape* is founded on the idea that the abandoned lots or untended fragments of the Planetary Garden are the refuge of terrestrial biodiversity, and that our biological future can be found here. Spaces of this type exist everywhere in the world"[14].

The rigorous scientific approach of GC does not prevent, but even perhaps implies and requires, an inevitable shift onto social terrain. Our future (ecological, but also political) lies in the leftovers, the uncontrolled spaces, the abandoned areas, the interstices of freedom that escape the fate of dedicated space entirely subjected to social control. The future, the hope and wealth of all, lie precisely in that biological and spatial reserve that comes from rejection and abandonment, in the residual zone that manages to find shelter, beyond interests, beyond the margins of the economic apparatus. Protected by its own lack of value, such space invents an alternative form of life.

GC's gaze, as it expresses itself in the observatory/laboratory of La Vallée, apparently focuses exclusively on natural phenomena, and I believe that in his many writings there is never a hint of parallels with the society of men. There is often urging toward direct commitment, in the ecological and therefore political sense, but the natural ecology never translates into social ecology. Though the borderline may seem flexible, at times, the discussion always remains silent with respect to a subject that seems to be there, at arm's reach, but is never called into play. GC expects us, his readers and commentators, to be able to interpret and transfer his key words and reasoning into other areas.

After all, the most fertile ideas are precisely those that lend themselves to misunderstanding and exploitation. Availability for dissemination and genetic mutation is the best demonstration of their intelligence and vitality. For example, the Lamarckian radicalism of GC, based on an idea of continuous, interdependent evolution of

LANDSCAPE AND GARDEN

"The landscape sends back each of its perspectives to the inner perspectives of its observer. The garden is a demonstration of thought. The landscape, a cultural symptom, creation of the spirit, will be nothing without its own image, achieved and acquired through the body: the garden. Every man, subjected to his own cosmogony, keeps a garden inside him that translates the landscape and, in the background, the entire universe. The fact that the visible and the invisible coexist in a controlled, circumscribed place of nature forces us to consider this place, the garden, as the specialized territory of the soul, where artifice, whatever its abilities and results, is at the service of more distant visions. Thus the impossibility of limiting this place to its physical confines. The correlation between landscape and garden happens when man becomes aware of his environment and finds the words to define it."

the nomadic garden, the permanent traveller

species, represents a third position in the ecological debate, one that does not belong either to conservatives or to modernists. Yet it is easy to imagine how the slogans of GC could be utilized to support opposing strategies. Strict ecologists could use them as effective weapons against the industrialization of agriculture and the irresponsible consumption of the great planetary reserves of Third Landscape. Anti-ecologists could easily find many points to support non-conservation, change and even naturalistic globalization, which according to GC has brought the planet, today, to a climax of wealth and biodiversity.

The planetary, nomadic and libertarian vision of GC has clear similarities to the viewpoint of Bruce Chatwin, the great art expert and brilliant traveller (as well as a very attentive reader of Deleuze's and Guattari's *Mille plateaux*), who invented a new, immediately comprehensible and fascinating way of crossing and narrating the planet for readers all over the world. In *The Songlines*, the "dream tracks" through which Native Australians encode every corner of the continent in words, Chatwin presents himself as a traveller in a world of travellers, taking part in a planet in movement in which transit, passage, migration and nomadism are the best and most authentic representations of life itself. For Chatwin's expert gaze, the Planetary Garden is an immediately perceptible reality in every corner of our little world: "A late summer evening in Manhattan, the crowds out of town, cycling down lower Park Avenue with the light slanting in from the cross-streets and a stream of monarch butterflies, alternately brown in the shadow and golden in the sun, coming round the Pan Am building, descending from the statue of Mercury on Grand Central Station and continuing downtown towards the Caribbean"[15].

RECENT PROJECTS

The entire œuvre of GC can be seen as a practice that is hard to compare to the positions expressed by other landscape designers. The differences are many, above all an absolutely particular relationship with the visible. To simplify, we might say that the occidental garden is first of all a place of views, of panoramas, scenes, glimpses and perspectives. This assumption remains a formidable force even in today's leading landscape architecture. The principles of classical composition may have been abandoned, but the primacy of the visible, and therefore the principle of composition based on the viewpoint of the observer, seems to maintain its central role. The contemporary garden still and first of all remains a sensorial arrangement based on sight, joined by the contribution of the other senses, that perceive the aromas of the plants, the sounds and tactile qualities of vegetation, wind and water. Traditional and innovative man-made materials – timber, stone, concrete, steel, asphalt, resins, paints – are integrated in this context without producing any particular friction. But with GC a completely new garden appears, the first not conceived in terms of the human presence, where man is a visitor amongst other living visitors, plants and animals, a presence not necessary and at times even to exclude, as on the Derborence island in Parc Matisse. GC's garden is a region in which man has limited sovereignty, and it

THE GARDEN

"It welcomes plants, animals, man and his dreams. It is a voyage, a walk. Landscapes accumulate there and the path grows, passing from one universe to the other. Transitions abound: from an orchard to a vegetable patch, from a flower garden to a meadow, from a labyrinth to a wood, from a green room to a belvedere, from the courtyard to the street. Not one of these places can be said to be unlimited, and no path can happen without passageways and gates. Tradition excludes from the garden all those living species, animals or plants, that defy the gardener's control. The advent of ecology overturns this view. By principle, it is interested in nature as a whole, not in the garden. Yet the garden is made of nature. Birds, ants, mushrooms, insects and seeds do not recognize the borders that separate land tamed by police-like control and untended, wild land. For them, any place is inhabitable."

the nomadic garden, the permanent traveller

is this limitation of his powers that produces the mystery, the enigmatic exoticism, the incomparable charm of these places.

The projects illustrated in this book provide a significant overview of almost four decades of activity, which proceeding amidst multiple experiences, interests and different places, now reaches the point of expressing, in a clear, exhaustive way, a complete vision. There are many other projects in progress, which will be marked by his typical forceful experimental thrust, but it is possible to take stock, today, of the level achieved over the last decade, the apex of a trajectory that has aspects of great originality and may serve as a point of reference of great, fertile evocative power for all design culture. Fulfilling the message of GC would indeed represent a true Copernican revolution, starting at its point of origin, the Garden in Movement. If the gardener observes, accompanies and follows the (more or less) spontaneous movement of the garden, what becomes of the idea of landscape design? The gap is clear, and design finds itself out of step, in an irreversible way. Yet one distinction must be made. There is formal design, that imposes a relationship with nature based on total domination, in the selection and arrangement of plants and the necessary manipulation of the land. This design works on the basis of a heavily selective treatment of the land, of severe control of the living world, including the animals, and of the permanence of the order it institutes. But there is also a different, alternative kind of design, one that is harder to define, that addresses the permanent part of the garden, what we might call the infrastructure, and guarantees respect for basic necessities: access, internal paths, wellbeing and safety, both for visitors and for the living things of the garden. In certain projects, at Rayol and in Parc Matisse, this design is limited to a few, very significant episodes: the steps, the paths, the ecological island. We can sense the echo of the experience of the experimental garden of La Vallée. These are the most radical demonstrations, where the skill and experimental taste of the gardener are most evident. In the projects of Blois and Valloires, the relationship with the historical buildings is reflected in a reworking of traditional figures – the esplanade, the grotto, the promenade, the flight of steps, the perspective axis – which are treated in a utilitarian way, stripped of their monumental emphasis and reinforced in their functional aspects, for the organization and layout of spaces.

THE PLANETARY INDEX

"The garden, seen in the traditional perspective, is a place that encourages planetary mingling. Every garden, inevitably adorned with species from every corner of the globe, can be considered a planetary index. And every gardener is an intermediary facilitating encounters between species that seemed to be destined never to meet. Planetary mingling, originally regulated by the natural action of the elements, is enriched by the contribution of human activity, which is in constant expansion. The range of man's intervention determines the level of control of the territory subjected to his management. In the garden, while everything may not be controlled, it is still known. Neglected species, in the garden, are intentionally overlooked, for convenience or necessity, but neglected space is not necessarily unknown space. The planet, entirely subjected to satellite surveillance, is comparable to a garden, in this sense. The Planetary Garden is a way of interpreting ecology, including man, the gardener, in the least important of his spaces. The philosophy that defines it is directly derived from the Garden in Movement: 'to do as much as possible with, and as little as possible against'. The objective of the Planetary Garden is to pursue development of maximum diversity without destroying it. The goal is: how to continue to make the planetary 'machine' function, how to make the garden live and, therefore, the gardener as well."

the nomadic garden, the permanent traveller

On other occasions, as in the gardens of the Arche de La Défense and those of the Quai Branly museum, the matrix of the Garden in Movement ceases to be an insert, a theme, and penetrates the very nature of the project. Under the steel walkway of La Défense GC imagines a powerful landscape, free of any formal conditioning. The only and determining design element is the paving, made with rocks and inserts of stone slabs, in an irregular, crafted approach, artfully separated to allow freedom of movement for the roots of the trees, and ready to be colonized by mosses. Reminders of spontaneous architecture, of Italian historical centres, perhaps, and maybe also of the extraordinary paving of the climb to the Acropolis in Athens, installed by Dimitris Pikionis in 1954-57. The garden of Quai Branly, which will be even more effective when the vegetation has grown, offers yet another version. The overall layout is more naturalistic and informal, free of dominant orientations or axes, while much of the design work concentrates on the details: paths, borders, supports, paving and even abstract decorative elements that frame nature in a subordinate landscape, with respect to the presence of the museum building designed by Jean Nouvel, yet also a landscape dense with artificial inserts of great plastic and material presence. A separate discussion should be devoted to the Parc André Citroën, the work responsible for GC's popularity, though the project was developed in tandem by the two teams that won the competition, ex-aequo: one formed by the architect Patrick Berger and GC, the other formed by the architects Viguier and Jodry with the landscape designer Alain Provost. The two groups worked together on the definitive project, subdivided along its main axis: the southern side,

IN PRAISE OF VAGABONDS

"The movements of animals correspond, generally, to the voyage. Those of plants, generally, correspond to wandering. The wandering of species produces surprising effects: for example, botanists had not envisioned the 'urban' category of ecology. Plants travel, especially the herbs. They move in silence, carried by the winds and by chance, which organizes the details and uses all the possible vectors, from marine currents to the soles of shoes. Let's think of the multiplicity of encounters and the diversity of living beings as wealth factors. Let's observe life in its dynamic evolution, with its usual share of amorality. I do not judge, but I take sides in favour of those energies capable of inventing new situations that, probably, are to the detriment of diversity. The variety of configurations vs. the diversity of living beings, although one certainly does not prevent the other."

the nomadic garden, the permanent traveller

part of the central space, the canal, the garden of metamorphoses and the black garden were assigned to Provost – Viguier – Jodry; the northern side, the Garden in Movement, the evening gardens, the large greenhouses and the white garden to the duo Berger – Clément. The results are spectacular, generating at the time the first large urban park in a European city designed according to contemporary criteria. Precisely in Paris, in 1982, the competition for Parc de la Villette had pushed aside the idea of an urban park based on the central role of natural elements. The winning and completed project, that of Bernard Tschumi, was based on the architectural variations of the 35 "folies", small metal constructions, painted red, arranged on a regular grid to punctuate the large parterre crossed by a canal and a suspended footbridge. Ten years later, Patrick Berger returned to the idea of the "folies", but transformed the constructions into greenhouses. This new development, or reversal of direction, signalled the new central role of the botanical component. Though organized within a very strong architectural system, the design of the vegetation managed to come to the fore and assert itself as the most innovative aspect of the park. The Garden in Movement, placed near

the most often used entrance, caused controversy even before it was built, but then established itself as the most interesting and utilized part of the complex, capable of attracting a greater number of visitors than any other sector. To the side, along the parterre, extends a very eloquent sequence of serial or thematic gardens, which are perhaps the most fully designed, classical and photogenic of all the works of GC, as well as the work of most immediate impact. Today the Parc Citroën, with the esplanade, central axis, refined details and the two larger greenhouses, monumental like two temples, may seem like a necessary passage, a transition phase leading to a more informal future. In the more recent projects the relationship between design and nature seems to be more mobile and flexible, freed of traditional aesthetic canons, projected into an evolutionary course whose end cannot yet be imagined. The garden regains the characteristics of sacredness and simplicity that make it important and necessary: the work of GC continues to open up new perspectives, harbingers of landscapes that have yet to be explored.

ALESSANDRO ROCCA

CLIMAX

"In botanical ecology the climax is the optimal level of vegetation for a given place. It can be a forest or a moor. Observing land that is moving towards its climax, we see all the constituent parts of the garden pass before our eyes, its archetypes and elements, all intertwined with each other in keeping with a biological destiny that, case by case, protects or destroys them. What we can observe in untended territory sums up all the problems of the garden and the landscape: movement. To ignore this movement means seeing the plant as a finite object, and it also means historically and biologically isolating it from the context that permits its existence."

Year 0-1

Abandoned land. Presence of a few, occasional plants.

Years 1-3

If the land is of agricultural origin, a meadow is directly formed. Otherwise, first a
layer of mosses takes form, and then, later, a grassy covering.

Years 3-7

The meadow is interrupted by colonizing shrubs, mostly thorny plants. Armoured prairie.

Years 7-14

The meadow area diminishes, the shrubs increase.
In the midst of the brambles, safe from predators, the tall trees of the future sprout and grow.

Years 14-40

If the land is suitable, the growth of trees produces shade that causes the decline of the shrubs that protected those trees when they were still saplings; in other cases, the untended land may stop at an earlier stage.
In all cases, the vegetation corresponds to a climax, the optimal level of vegetation for a given place.

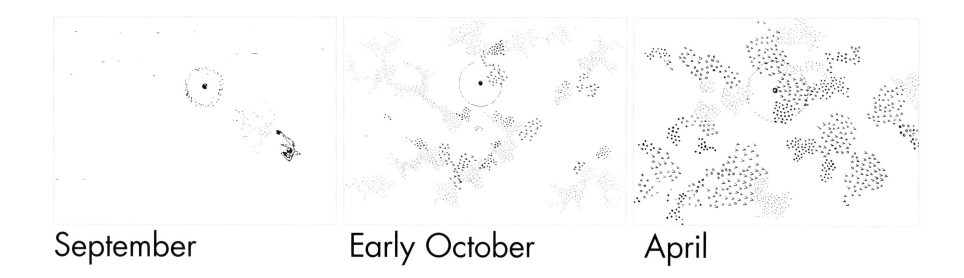

September

Early October

April

Sowing, and the little tree at the centre is already there, you like it.
il vous plaît.

The first seeds have sprouted. You can see the annuals and the gramineae, the biennials (future wanderers) and already a few perennials.

The soil is decidedly "firmer" than it was at the start of the winter. New species have appeared. The terrain starts to fill up. You look for the best way to make paths. The perennials have grown so much that you cannot conserve them all.

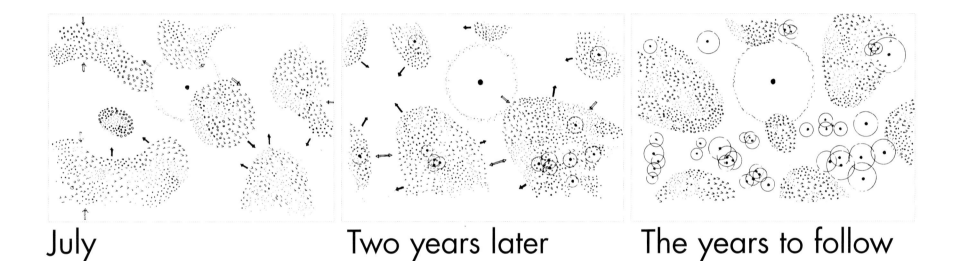

July

Two years later

The years to follow

With an appropriate machine, you have traced the contours of the islands. In certain parts the islands shrink, in other points they gain ground. The arrows indicate these movements.

The tree you liked so much shades the grass, which dies. Elsewhere, in the midst of the islands that have repeatedly changed their forms and proportions, young trees are growing. You are perplexed: the place is becoming a forest.

The size of the flowering islands has diminished. The shade of the young trees is still not strong enough to eliminate the grassy ground-cover, but it soon will be, and you have gone ahead, isolating the trees in the meadow. In one or two years you will have to decide: whether to remove them, for a return of light and flowers, or whether to let the woodland take form.

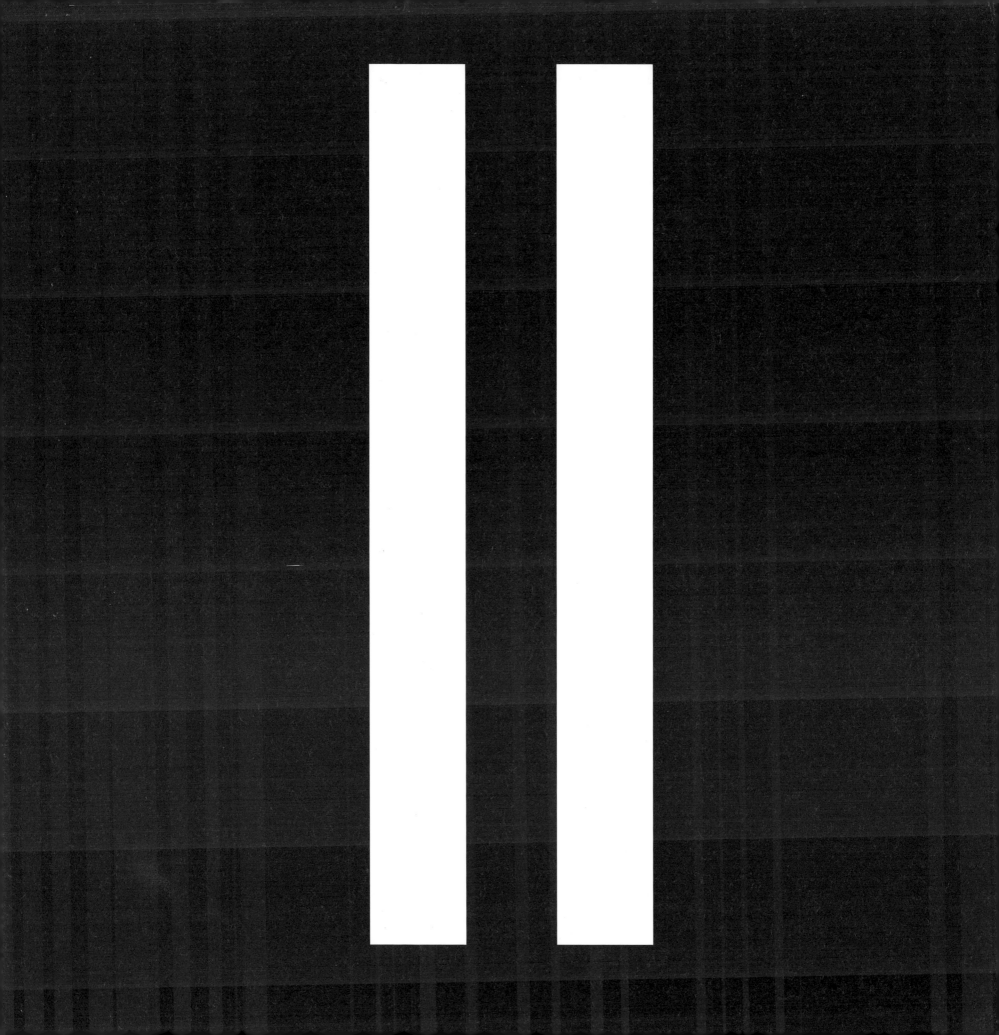

THE LAND-SCAPE IS A DETAIL OF THE GARDEN

CONVERSATION WITH GILLES CLÉMENT

ALESSANDRO ROCCA. We're at La Vallée, your experimental garden in the countryside of La Creuse, to talk about your projects, which for the most part are located in urban settings. How do you interpret the relationship between nature and city, and what do you think, for example, about the presence of animals in cities?

GILLES CLÉMENT. I think there isn't much difference between the country and the city, in the sense that today there are many possibilities for plants and animals to exist, together with humans, in cities, where strangely enough they often find very favourable conditions. In certain parts of the countryside, not here in La Creuse but in Berry, Champagne or Picardy, the biological variety of plants and animals has almost vanished, destroyed by pesticides and chemical treatments. So often the diversity is very limited in the country, whereas in cities we find a very high level of diversity. An example: Olivier Darné, a beekeeper and artist who raises bees in Saint-Denis, on the northern outskirts of Paris, has positioned the hives under the eaves of the town hall. His bees make exceptional, very pure honey, because it comes from a truly incredible number of different kinds of pollen. It is better than the honey you can find in the country, and equal to the honey made in the mountains, proving that this diversity exists, that it is vital and widely compatible, from a biological viewpoint. This fact indicates reason for hope. Traumatized places are easier to find in the countryside than in the city.

THE LIVING WORLD

A.R. In your gardens you grant great freedom to nature, while at the same time you design very strong architectural elements that set insuperable and, in a certain sense, also violent limits. I'm thinking about the Parc André Citroën, in Paris, and the Parc Henri Matisse in Lille. So there is a relationship among design, architecture and nature that can be organized on multiple, different levels.

G.C. You cannot limit nature, that's an illusion, the illusion and the vanity of the architect. This is my opinion, and I think that the design, and therefore the architect, exist to bring out the value of nature. Therefore I work in terms of contrast: if there is no form, if there are no designed paths, if there are no geometrically simplified elements, then you cannot understand what was being demonstrated, what was intended to be expressed. For example, you cannot comprehend and accept the apparently chaotic lushness of nature if this chaos is not staged, so to speak. On the Derborence island, in Parc Henri Matisse in Lille, we have made a setting for the work of nature, using nature itself. Otherwise the plateau on the hill would be nothing but untended land and the garden would remain incomprehensible. It is already hard to make people understand it as it is.

A.R. Valloires, Blois, Citroën: in your projects you use traditional design features: alignments and perspective backdrops, correspondences, symmetries, etc. How important is the heritage of the classic French garden in your thinking and your designs, and in what way is it important?

G.C. I do not refer to French Classicism, but to a notion of balance that is a specific characteristic of occidental culture and design; a balance achieved at times through symmetry, and in other cases through false symmetry. It is a work of point and counterpoint, a bit like Baroque music. In certain cases I introduce things that absolutely do not belong to our culture, that come from the orient, but I don't do that in a conscious way, they are influences that have been noticed by others, things I wasn't aware of.

THE SERIAL GARDENS
THE GARDEN IN MOVEMENT

A.R. Could you give us an example of these unconscious imports?

G.C. It's been said that the Silver Garden, one of the gardens of the Parc Citroën, is an oriental, Japanese garden. Of course it is not, but it does use particular relationships of value, of contrast between ground and vegetation. The texture and the arrangement of the plants in space may reflect, in some ways, certain styles of oriental gardens, though I am certain that no oriental person would recognize the place as oriental. So you undergo influences without realizing it, but that is not very important. Instead, what I am looking for is a correct response to a question posed by the place through its history, people, climate, soil. Sometimes the response makes it necessary for me to use the tools of history, like a perspective, or more generally a formal, classical construction. This happened to me with the cloisters of Valloires, in the project for the Parisian headquarters of Crédit Foncier, and in other situations in which I was surrounded by buildings, by a vividly present, very potent history and architecture, that demanded my collaboration, that I could not ignore. We *paysagistes* are in the *topos*, our utopia is not the denial of the *topos* but something else, a dream about the future, perhaps, one that takes all the facts of each place into account, because always the place has been built by men. This given must always be kept in mind: men are history.

A.R. The Parc Citroën is perhaps your most famous project, but it may also be the one that is least "yours", because the architectural design is by Patrick Berger and, as a whole, it is a complex story of different collaborations and contributions. The Serial Gardens, which are extraordinary, seem to me to be the result of a compositional effort you have not repeated since.

G.C. For me the Serial Gardens were a means to be able to make, in counterpoint, the Garden in Movement, which in contrast is completely without composition. The formal work is done by the gardener, in the spring, and every year the garden changes. The Serial Gardens, where there is a lot of composition work, are based on the English tradition, and also a bit on walled gardens. Maybe it is not correct to talk about a really traditional approach, but it is true that in order to maintain the gardens you need to do traditional gardening: removing weeds, pruning plants, etc. In this case I wanted to do a work of excellence, a stylistic exercise on the reassuring theme of the garden full of a controlled, tamed diversity. I wanted to demonstrate that while this is a part of our craft, today we can also approach the garden from another direction. In my view, one option does not destroy the other. Today, in France, more and more Gardens in Movement are being made, this way of working is becoming a definitive acquisition, and this is very positive, it's perfect. Both alternative modes are forms, but the question is not about form, it is about what you want to say; the problem of meaning becomes the truly important question.

A.R. I think that in the gardens of the Arche, at La Défense, you have reached a very advanced balance between design and nature, because somehow the importance of the design returns, enhanced by a more harmonious, more organic relationship with the Garden in Movement.

G.C. Certainly, and this was possible because the Parc Citroën, which marked a historical moment, came first. That was the first time it was possible to propose, in Paris, a very organic and very informal garden, really dominated, to a great extent, by nature itself. In the years to follow I could have sustained this proposal (the Garden in Movement) without the reassuring counterpart of the Serial Gardens, but at the time it was not possible. After the Parc Citroën opinions changed, clients understood that there were other ways of designing. I have been able to work with greater freedom, and so it has become easier to combine architecture and nature in a free enough way to allow nature to express itself. In my view, the Parc Matisse, after the gardens at the Arche, goes even further, and I believe it is my most contemporary, most advanced project.

A.R. On several occasions you have emphasized the importance and the need for landscape designers to have an in-depth knowledge of botany. What do you think about the training of landscape designers and how should a new school of landscape design be organized, today?

G.C. In France the training is quite advanced, generally, and at Versailles (the École Nationale Supérieure du Paysage, where I teach) it is also very good on the design level. But on the level of knowledge of the living world it is catastrophic. I believe the rest of Europe is even worse, except for some of the Nordic countries, where we find great awareness of the importance of the living world. Here in France we are seeing an enormous failure, and I never tire of repeating, at the start of every school year, that we need to create a place exclusively devoted to the teaching of basic scientific knowledge about the world of plants. It is equally necessary to know about insects, because the entomological world has great wealth that is totally dependent on the botanical world, while at the same time many animals depend entirely on insects to survive. Therefore insects form an interdependent system that works in both directions, between the plant and animal worlds, and an understanding of all this can be very helpful to fully comprehend the Planetary Garden and all those systems that can be called ecosystems. Consequently, we need to construct a new intelligence, so that the garden will no longer be considered an object, but something that lives, in time, through the care of the gardener, and therefore something that is closely connected to the life of plants, animals, the ecosystem. This is the essence of gardening, which unfortunately is all too often completely ignored. Sizeable resources are often involved in the creation of projects, but then there are no funds left to maintain them and to train gardeners with a knowledge of this complexity. It's terrible.

A.R. What role should architecture have in the training, as you see it?

G.C. I'm not sure how to say it, but I think that the void, i.e. open space that can be seen as being without edification, is the federating element: it puts together all the elements around it, which are often constructed elements. So there is a strong federative function, which urbanists can understand quite well, and which landscape designers generally understand very well, because this is the material with which they operate. Landscape designers work with open space and living things.

A.R. Looking at the past, at history and tradition, which gardens do you think are the most important?

G.C. I've had some surprises, some aesthetic shocks in my life, and I can compare certain gardens and landscapes in terms of their equal intensity. I cannot say that any one garden has influenced me in a direct way. There have been some, like the Sissinghurst Castle Garden in England, that have had a very strong, intense effect on me: it is an Edwardian garden that condenses that whole tradition, which is extremely rich in diversity, very cultured, elegant, absolutely seductive, and very daring from an intellectual viewpoint. I must say that when I have been in certain places, like Cradle Mountain, in Tasmania, or on the Pacific coast at La Serena, in Chile, the landscapes seemed like perfectly evolved, magnificent gardens, with relationships of tones, form, colours, materials, rocks that were so amazing as to leave me completely dumbfounded. I really can't make a ranking, to say which of these situations was better than others.

A.R. And what are the most interesting gardens today, in your view?

G.C. I think the most interesting gardens today are those made by unknown people, sometimes by very modest people. Here (in the village of Crozant, in the French region of La Creuse) there is a lady who has a very small garden, she probably doesn't know the names of the plants, at least not in scientific terms, but she understands them very well and knows why they are there. I know that some of her plants are difficult to manage, but she maintains them all in a very small space, organizing them in a composition of shade and light. She has flowers, fruit trees and vegetables, and her little garden is a mixture that demonstrates extreme respect for all the species it contains. This is a woman who has three goats, who makes cheese and lives on nothing; she is poor, though certainly not destitute, but on the level of knowledge of plants she is very erudite. In other situations you find many other people who have amazing little vegetable patches, people who work in cooperative gardens, the ones they call family gardens, or in Paris they call them shared gardens. These are not professionals, they are amateurs, enthusiasts. There are also therapeutic gardens, where specialists work with people who have problems, who are unemployed or in difficulty for other reasons, and in these contexts gardening is a part of the overall therapy. They are people who have been expelled from the society and return to life through the garden. For me these are the most beautiful gardens of all.

A.R. How do you imagine the garden of the future, and what will be the role of ecology?

G.C. I believe that gardens will either be ecological or they won't exist, the opposite is unimaginable. Nature has undergone a severe trauma, due to the mistreatment inflicted by toxic products that generates an economy supported by the lobbies of the big industrial corporations. This is happening in France, Europe and also in America. Certainly the situation is extremely serious and difficult, today, with the advent of new threats, such as bio-fuel, for example, which is a truly disturbing prospect. At the level of the garden there is a new awareness (the new awareness of ecological issues is also general) of the need to return to ecological methods, but the legislation does not move in the same direction because it protects the lobbies, on a national and a European level. France is way behind, laws for agriculture prohibit the use of untested products, and in practice they protect the business of the lobbies and the chemical industry. So I think the garden of tomorrow will be a garden that pays close attention to nature, a prudent place that uses ecological methods that can be categorized under the heading of so-called "biological gardening". Very simple, organic products do exist, that do not damage nature, that are not dangerous, things we can produce by ourselves in the home, or things that can be purchased through a commercial network that unfortunately is not supported at all. Today, I think, it can reach about 3% of the market. The situation is difficult and problematic, but in any case this is the path of the future.

A.R. Today landscape designers often work in the position of urban planners. Do you think this process is going to become established, producing a new balance among professional roles? Does this mean everything is landscape? Or, at least, that everything is part of the question of landscape?

G.C. This is truly an important question, because recently, in the 1960s and 1970s, the landscape dimension has entered the city, in urban planning and in people's thinking. The paths of the urbanist and the landscape designer, as I was saying before, are getting closer to each other, but the urbanist's reasoning starts with the layout of the city, while the landscaper starts with the idea of landscape, which means beginning with a combination of open and full space, nature and architecture. The main difference lies in the basic premises or assumptions. I believe the landscape has taken on great importance for people in general, and therefore projects on an urban scale have an increasing chance of being assigned to landscape designers. In France, two outstanding landscape designers like Alexandre Chemetoff and Michel Corajoud have received the Grand Prix de l'Urbanisme (respectively in 2000 and 2003), an unexpected honour but one that is justified by the fact that they have worked in this field.

A.R. For example, in the design of infrastructures and new residential or industrial settlements, isn't there the danger that a landscape designer will approach the task in terms of beautification, instead of working on the real organization of the territory?

G.C. In effect the danger is there, but it is a risk that would also arise with any urban planner who has the ideas of a decorator, or with architects who know nothing about the environment and may tend to have the sole objective of building a beautiful object. Architects very frequently make interesting, attractive objects, while failing to pay attention to their harmonious insertion in a larger spatial context. So the danger depends enormously on the person and his or her ability to analyze and comprehend. There is always the risk of a purely aesthetic approach, in all the professions.

A.R. How do you work, and how should a landscape designer work, when operating in a landscape without nature, a completely artificial place, a typically urban environment?

G.C. What counts is truly the question of meaning. When I have to design a square I ask myself who will come there, for whom is it being made, and at that point one realizes that in these cases the design is exclusively for human beings. Very rarely is there any questioning about the landscape in which people are not seen as the main beneficiaries. This may happen in the natural environment, where it is possible to imagine places forbidden to humans, but that is an extreme case. So we ask ourselves if people will rest there, stroll there in the evening, meet, make love; these are fundamental things, and without them we cannot live. So the idea develops of a landscape that takes on meaning in relation to people, in relation to the human beings that will live there. Sometimes the meaning comes from another question, for instance when there is such a strong historical presence at the site that it is impossible not to take it into account.

A.R. Actually, even in a totally constructed environment nature is always there, at least in the form of humans.

G.C. Exactly.

A.R. What weight do political reflections and commitment have in your theoretical and practical work?

G.C. In the beginning I absolutely didn't imagine that political reflection would be necessary, but gradually, as I began to work less on private projects and more in public spaces, I had to accept the evidence and I realized that the political question was essential. Today I see that I have become more radical, in the sense that I have taken a political position that can be seen as an ecological project. I believe it can be a possible starting point from which to construct a new society. Obviously it is a utopia, but the Planetary Garden is a very concrete, very realistic utopia, and basically quite modest, because its operative goals are specific, localized usage modes, very close to the work of Alberto Magnaghi. This year I discovered his book *Il progetto locale*, and I was struck by his way of thinking about places in relation to a certain economy of energies, expressing a conception that corresponds to the ecological sense of environmental protection and is informed, at the same time, by thinking on a planetary scale. This is precisely the idea of the Planetary Garden I had developed in 1999 and even earlier (I wrote *Thomas et le voyageur* in 1996, but at the time the concept had not completely taken form). So I cannot understand why politicians have not been attracted by this concept, why they do not use it to make a project. I have brought visitors to the exhibition on the *Jardin planétaire* (at the Grande Halle de la Villette, Paris, 1999-2000) like Lionel Jospin (when he was prime minister), Dominique Voynet (minister of the territory and the environment) and others who had important positions of responsibility, who were really running the country, and for example I can say that Dominique Voynet was aware of the importance of these arguments, but did not have the means to come to grips with them. Today (on the eve of the presidential elections) Voynet is in the running, but unfortunately she is supported only by the Green party. I would vote for her, I admire her because I think she has made fundamental choices that she was not able to apply because she was prevented from going forward. For example, her important initiatives on combined rail/truck transport and transport on water were stopped or cancelled by the government of which she was a part.

A.R. What is the importance, if any, of literary reflections in your work?

G.C. I don't know if it is possible to speak of literary reflections, but the question of writing is fundamental. I do not have thoughts on literature, but on writing. I think that every time one begins to write, one is obliged to choose the words, and this is a considerable commitment that requires us to be perfectly clear with a few words, few shadings, removing useless things, to get where we want to go. It is also an exercise that helps to clarify thinking, no other exercise is so effective. I ask my students, after they have imagined a project, to describe it, in two pages. Often after they have described it they change it, because they have realized, through writing, that in their imagination there were incompatible things that had to be reconciled, contradictions that would not have become evident without the practice of writing. At that point they can eliminate what needs eliminating and keep what needs keeping, and things fall into place. So it is an incredibly efficient exercise of distilling, eliminating what is useless.

A.R. I have the impression of a very well-gauged balance between your personal dimension, that of solitary writing and entomology, observation of nature and private gardening at La Vallée, and your activities of relations, like the teaching at the school of Versailles, the lectures, the very active participation in public life and in the cultural and political debate. Do these two parts of your experience find a meeting point in the practice of design, and is the differentiated handling of the garden comparable to this situation of dualism?

G.C. Yes, perhaps there is a similarity I haven't been aware of. Here in my garden at La Vallée I feel, and I am, in direct relation with the complexity of the living world; in society, I relate to the complexity of the living world only through people. I'm certain there is a similarity, in the sense that I believe that I bring the same respect to other living things – plants and animals – and to human beings, in their cultural, ethnic and physical diversity. I need to really feel that I am being attacked, with great violence, to put myself in a position of conflict against another person, or against an animal. In effect, in the differentiated tending of the garden there is the same concern with preserving diversity, and this is also true for the planetary mixture, just as in my relationship with society there is the concern to approach everyone without discrimination, something that can be very arduous at times. Finding a balance is complicated, laborious, always as a result of humans. Plants and animals don't make demands.

THE SYMBIOTIC MAN

A.R. After the Garden in Movement, the Planetary Garden and the Third Landscape, what is the idea, the theory, the thought that still hasn't come to you, something you feel a need for, on which you are working?

G.C. I'm working on a proposition I am not sure I will be able to demonstrate; I call it "the symbiotic man". The idea is based on the conviction that we are headed toward a sort of economic and ecological catastrophe that will generate a condition of de-growth and, therefore, a totally different economics. Having reached the crisis, it will be time to search for a remedy, a cure, the medicine to cure the earth of all the harm done to it, to restore biological equilibrium, if that is still possible. In the foreseeable scenario, and with the world population constantly growing, life will have to be organized in a new way, with new ideas and new tools, and I imagine that this condition can be summed up in the idea of the symbiotic man. Because we take everything from the environment – everything comes from it, everything we have, all that we eat and breathe; we are totally dependent on the environment for our life – and it is clear that by living we destroy it, the opposite has to happen: by living, we have to restore something to the environment. If we live in symbiosis, all the benefits we receive must correspond to benefits we restore to the environment. If we can achieve this exchange, we will truly be in a state of symbiosis, in keeping with the model of change I call the "symbiotic man". I don't know how this can work, we are still far away from such a model, but we must make an attempt.

A.R. In your experience, who understands your ideas best? Citizens, politicians, artists, architects?

G.C. Those with the best understanding of my positions are, to start with, the citizens, because I speak the language of the gardener, and many of them understand it. Next come the artists, who immediately understand because even if they do not know much about gardens or ecology, they can sense that something important lies there. Artists have always been the ones who question the world and its way of thinking, and my practice is similar to this approach. So the world of art has quickly understood that my path is close to that of the artist, and they have no problem with that.
The politicians understand nothing, or almost nothing, because they have been trained in a mentality that makes them full of certainties, and even if they have doubts once in a while, they have to behave very confidently, and this makes them close themselves off from the world. Often they have technocratic backgrounds, and above all they have never learned anything about the living world. Once they brought a politician here, to La Vallée, and I tried asking him to name the things in a very simple piece of nature. He was stumped, no one had ever taught him those names, or maybe it was too long ago and he had forgotten everything. This is a serious problem, because these people are running things, are responsible for everything, and they know absolutely nothing. Of course there are exceptions; Dominique Voynet is one of them.

A.R. The garden undoubtedly belongs to the world of art. Can you describe your relationship with contemporary art?

G.C. My relationship with contemporary art is ambivalent. There are artists I feel very close to because they are restless about the world, they feel an honest, real concern that is not a game or a trick. Then there are the cynical ones, who have understood very well that you can play with art and do clever, nimble things, but for me those things are totally without interest. There are lots of these cynics, and they make a lot of money. At times the more interesting artists are well-known and can make a decent living, but many of them are unknown and make no money, and this is one characteristic of the contemporary art world I don't like. I know artists of great force and talent who have not had the luck of being supported by an agent, or by the mass media, and I know others who have reached the heights of success in spite of the fact that they are catastrophically bad artists, and their success continues because they have media backing.

A.R. Are there any artists with whom you would like to work?

G.C. Definitely. I haven't thought much about this, but there is one Italian artist I really like: Giuliano Mauri. He has managed to do something that is extremely difficult, namely to charge forms and objects that could be ridiculous, from the vernacular, apparently easy to approach, with great poetic power. They are beautiful precisely for this reason. But working together is something else again. Today these artists very often work in space, so there is an absolute need for the project to be conceived by the artist and the landscape designer together, at the same time. Otherwise you would just put contemporary art objects, usually sculptures, in spaces that have no relation to them.

A.R. Getting back to the Parc Citroën: you collaborated with Patrick Berger on a competition project and, later, for your part of the garden. Judging from the results and from your writings, it would seem to have been a positive, productive relationship. Yet I don't think you have worked in the same way with another architect since then.

G.C. I have never had another collaboration as interesting as the one with Patrick Berger, and I regret not being able to continue working with him. Unfortunately there was a phenomenon of media coverage of the park that gave me greater visibility, because of the Garden in Movement, and this led to complaints from the other landscape designer (Alain Provost) and the architects (Patrick Berger and the studio of Jean-Paul Viguier and Jean-François Jodry). It certainly wasn't my fault, it was the fault of the journalists, I wrote letters and did what I could but it was no use, in the end the message that came through was that I was the sole creator of the park. Patrick Berger resented this and felt hurt, he wanted to be the star, it's normal, and he certainly couldn't have been pleased that somebody else stole the show. We haven't worked together since, but in any case his way of thinking taught me a lot and it was a very interesting collaboration.

A.R. Are there any architects that interest you particularly?

G.C. One day I would like to do a project with Renzo Piano. In my view he is the most amazing architect, today, in the occidental world. Every time he starts over, from zero, he never repeats himself and he doesn't like facile things, he is truly intelligent, I think he is extraordinary, a true artist.

A.R. You simultaneously practice many different forms of knowledge and expression: botany, entomology, landscape design, writing. Your work on the garden is the result of all these practices combined in your personality and your professional profile. How many Gilles Cléments are there? And which one runs the show?

G.C. I think the chief is the one who favours and respects this diversity of types of knowledge and behaviour. I don't put being a writer first, nor do I feel that I am principally a landscape designer, or a draftsman (actually I don't draw very well). Gilles lives in the complexity of life and it is society that tries to simplify things, out of convenience, or laziness, because it is more practical for governing and taxing to be able to say "he is an architect", or "he is a dentist". But it's not true, that guy could be both those things. He might also be a gardener, a pianist or something else. It's not impossible. This complexity must be respected because when a human being is reduced to just one label, just one function, it is a disturbing situation, and he also gets depressed, because he doesn't identify with that reality. This is why people take vacations, to think about something different. And this is why I never go on vacation.

A.R. Is this multiplicity a personal characteristic, or does it have a wider meaning?

G.C. Human beings are fundamentally complex, so when things are simplified we are looking at a pathological situation.

A.R. I think this discussion is also closely related to the question of technique: when the technical level increases it somehow demands specialization and reduces multiplicity, and this is a fact with which we must come to terms in contemporary society. So what is your relationship with technique?

G.C. I am involved in a few "technical" fields: gardening, writing, a bit of drawing, which I don't practice enough, and entomological manipulation, which I have abandoned because I no longer do classification and collection, which was a very technical activity indeed. Every time I approach these fields I try to do my best, and I can say that I am both a gardener and a writer, technically, but I am not an entomologist because I have not worked enough on this, I have the basic notions but I am lacking in other knowledge and updating. In my design work, when I see that there are technical problems or shortcomings I look for experts who, in turn, are not just pure and simple specialists.

A.R. How do you approach technology and the new perspectives it introduces in the natural environment?

G.C. Technology is fascinating because it is something that has the aim of helping us: sometimes it helps us and often it is a threat. I just got back from three days in Ardèche, where I am designing a wooden platform that will be lowered, like a well, into the rock. The work is very complicated, very technical, it requires a special technology because the usual tools are not capable of doing jobs like this. In the end, for example, we had to avoid electric saws and all modern utensils, and do everything by hand, as in the past. This happens because there are actions in which modern technology cannot replace the techniques of the past, but what is very interesting about technology is that it is very useful for some things and for others not. I have done an analysis and found that in the home there is only one indispensable machine, the washing machine, while all the others are completely useless, they are good for almost nothing. In the office nothing can take the place of the computer, which is admirable for the work that it does. But the effectively useful actions done with computers are very few in comparison to the enormous quantity of useless actions performed. We really do spend too much time in front of computers. There is also the question of how to utilize all this technology, and of how easy it is to become slaves of high technology: through fascination, laziness, inertia. This is a real trap. I know of houses where the attics are full of fantastic machines that were used for just three days and then became immediately obsolete, useless. It is a question of discernment: what's it for? Why? This is very important.

BIOTECHNOLOGIES

A.R. What do you think about biotechnologies, genetic manipulation, everything that imposes traumatic changes on the living world?

G.C. I think living things never stop doing biotechnology, without us, without man-made genetic modification of organisms (GMO): they are the result of an evolution that consists of the fabrication of something that continuously changes. In the end it is very banal, biotechnology and men are discovering something that nature has always done and continues to do. The difference lies in the objectives: we manipulate living organisms for our ends, organisms that would otherwise never have changed in those ways. We put a strawberry gene in a rabbit or in corn and we don't know what we are doing from a biological viewpoint. These are very strange manipulations and they are undoubtedly possible, since we can do them, but they are not aimed at helping strawberries or rabbits or corn, they are aimed at helping man, and therefore they are uncertain manipulations. All species have been transformed over time, they are GMOs that have fabricated their genetic modification to survive: when they are attacked by something, when there is external pressure, they react by adjusting themselves. This is a very frequent behaviour of trees, which cannot run away from animals or from changing conditions, so they have to react in another way. It is a typical, banal question of the living world, which is always orientated toward survival in time and the evolution of every species. We do something quite different, without the possibility of verifying the results of our action. We cannot know the consequences.
Nevertheless, I am an optimist, and I tell myself that the environment, meaning the complexity of the ecosystem, can adjust itself, reset itself, rebalance itself in spite of genetic modifications. What is even more dangerous is the way in which we use GMOs, it is really horrible, because with these manipulations the big laboratories take half, or perhaps all, of the human population hostage, forcing the consumption of modified products, stimulating their sale and prohibiting other products. The result is that they keep growing these modified plants that kill or sterilize, and in perspective they could reach the point of destroying the life of the planet. So we are seeing the progressive acquisition of a monopoly on the part of a few companies over the entire planet, to the detriment of the diversity of species and behaviours, and of the possibility of also inventing new things… It has become a grave planetary problem and the GMOs can be criticized not so much for what they are as for the way they are marketed and the policies regarding patents. This is the real problem.

A.R. Carlo Petrini, the founder of Slow Food, has promoted an interesting initiative to approach the problem of bio-technological patents. He has proposed constructing an online data bank in which to transcribe the history and characteristics of traditional seeds, the collective legacy of farmers all over the world. Once the seeds have been registered on a public website it would no longer be possible to patent them, thus blocking the process of conquest and monopolization of world agriculture on the part of multinational corporations.

G.C. This is what the research laboratories should be doing, working not to patent living things but to prevent them from being patented. It's a good idea. They should make him the prime minister of Italy!

LANDSCAPE AND GARDEN

A.R. In popular culture the landscape and the garden are two very different things. Landscape refers to something to look at, a concept that comes from painting; the garden, on the other hand, is a naturalistic microcosm completely designed and dominated by man. How would you explain the relationship between landscape and garden?

G.C. It is clearly a difficult question, but because I have often been asked about it I have been forced to think it through. In my view, the garden contains landscape. And today, starting with my vision of the earth as a planetary garden, it is even clearer to me that the landscape is a detail of the garden. But I have also defined landscape as follows: I say that it is everything that can be perceived by our gaze, and therefore everything that we see, and for those who do not have the sense of sight, everything that appears to them through the other senses. And it is also, above all, that which is conserved in memory, after closing your eyes, for example, or after covering your ears. It is a personal impression that depends on our culture, our way of observing, of seeing, of perceiving. So our interpretation is both cultural and individual, and as a result it is hard to share with people from distant cultures, and sometimes even with people from nearby cultures, because especially in the case of emotional involvement the individual dimension can easily prevail. The garden is something completely different, because it is a dream, it embodies a utopian vision. The garden is an ideal, it is Eden, and therefore it is something one protects, designs and organizes in keeping with the way one sees the world. With the passing of time the garden is inhabited by always different landscapes that are interpreted in different ways, depending on the people who find themselves in the garden.

A.R. Is this why you prefer to call yourself a gardener, instead of a landscape designer?

G.C. Yes, definitely. When I say that the garden is the only place of encounter between nature and man, the place where dreams are authorized, it is because I think the ideal is important, that which one believes is best. And though it is true that one can make mistakes, and probably will make them, it doesn't really matter. There is something that drives me on, that puts me in the situation of seeing a perspective, a goal projected in the future, and that indicates the direction in which to go. The landscape does not belong to all this, it is passive; landscape is just something to look at.

NINE
PLANETARY
GARDENS

BLOIS BRANLY MATISSE
VALLOIRES DRAC
CITROËN LA VALLÉE
RAYOL ARCHE

ARCADE, GROTTO AND PARTERRE AT
CHÂTEAU BLOIS

GARDENS OF CHÂTEAU BLOIS, 1989-1992
Gilles Clément, landscape designer
Antoine Debré, architect
Associate landscape designer:
Atelier Acanthe, Laurent Campos-Hugueney
1.5 hectares

The parking garage during construction, and the yew hedge garden.

Drawing showing the layout of the hedges and two views of the lower garden, at the time of planting and in a later phase. The garden stands out for the continuous movement of the waves of greenery, formed by yew hedges aligned with the school building and shaped at varying heights. The taller perennials are inserted in the midst of the hedges.

Anemones in bloom.

The pattern of the yew hedges with the terrace and the flights of steps that enclose the amethyst grotto, and the historic school building.

The royal flower terrace.

The officinal herb garden and the hornbeam arcade bordering the royal flower terrace on the middle level.

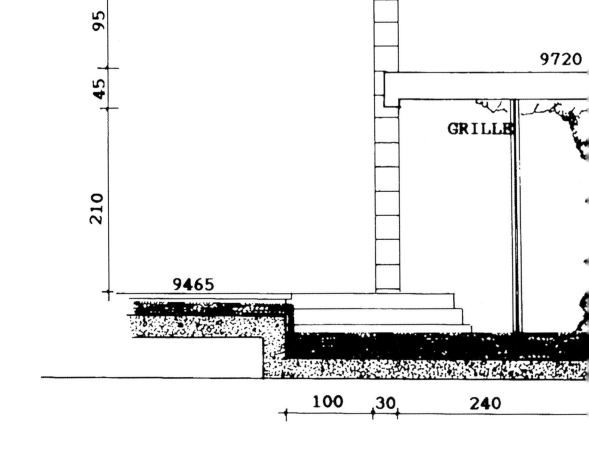

GRILLE

95

45

210

9465

100 30 240

At the centre of the royal flower terrace, between the flights of steps, the amethyst grotto is part of a hydric system in which each level contains at least one body of water. The water seeps from the wall and falls on crystals of calcite and amethyst. The fountain, with its baroque appearance, refers to the night, imagining the absolute blackness at the centre of a crystal geode suddenly exposed to the effects of light and weather.

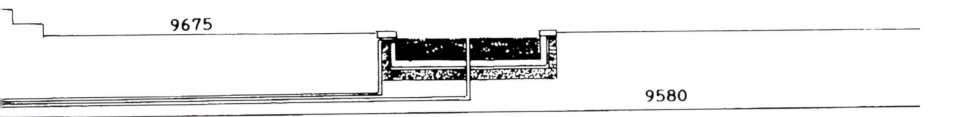

REMENT: CRISTAUX DE CALCITES

ET D'AMETHYSTES

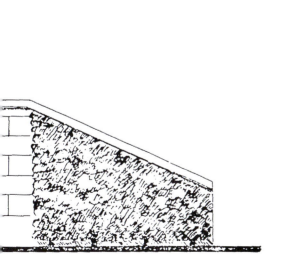

Detail, section and elevation of the grotto and the double flight of steps.

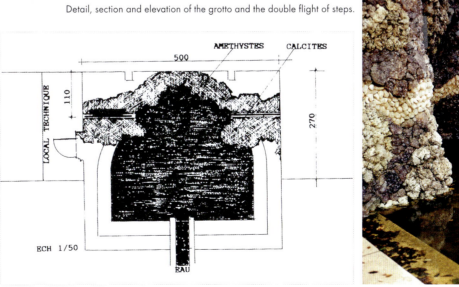

AROUND THE QUAI BRANLY

MUSEUM

BRANLY

GARDENS OF THE QUAI BRANLY MUSEUM, PARIS, 2005-2006
Gilles Clément
Associate landscape designers:
Atelier Acanthe, Nicolas Gilsoul, Emmanuelle Blanc
18.000 square metres

A. Théâtre de verdure
B. Moss garden
C. Clematis clearing
D. Rambling rose terrace
E. Candi clearing
F. Riviera of Rue de l'Université
G. Turtle gardens

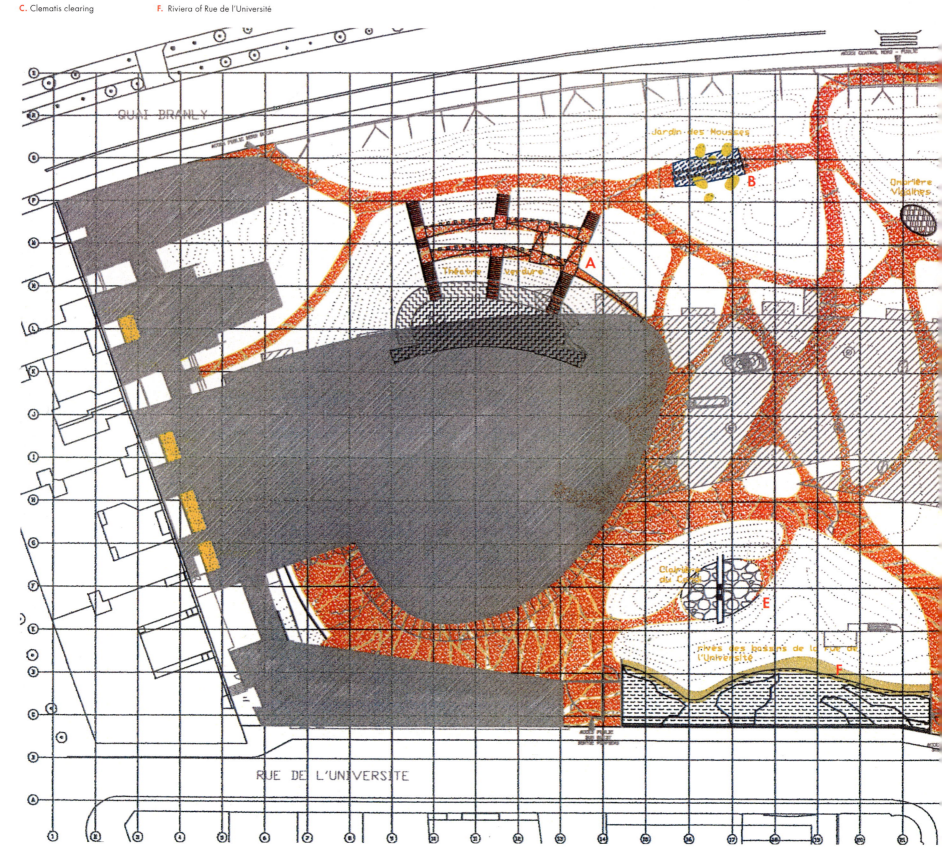

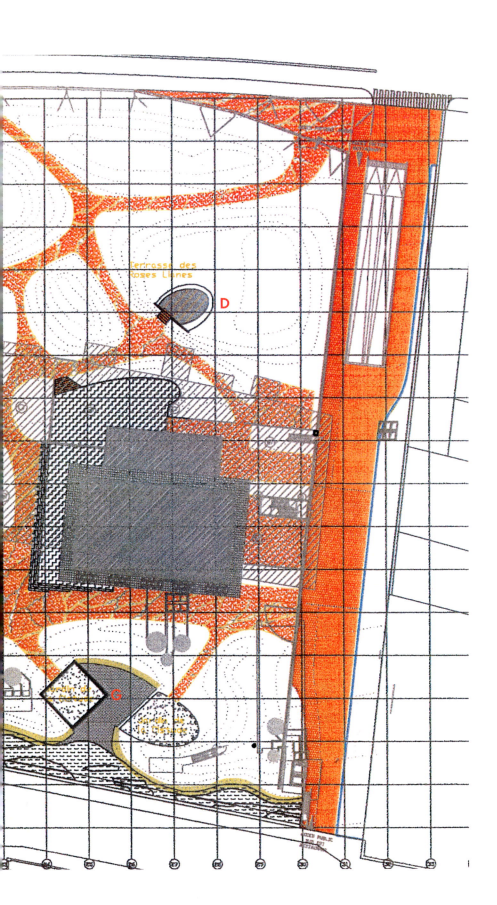

PLAN WITH PAVING SPECIFICATIONS

Cobbled joints in gneiss, ochre, beige, light grey.
Bush-hammered concrete poured on site with glass inserts. Light yellow finish
on white cement base. Crushed aggregate in beige, white and black.

Black bituminous asphalt.

Granite paving, 10x10 cm.

Granite border.
Candi (Bali, Indonesia) stone paving.
Large slate slabs and strips of blue-black schist.
Cistude (European lake turtle) clearing.
Crushed flat roofing tiles on thickness of 12 cm.

Red sienna terracotta.
Paving of the wild clematis house
in gneiss slabs with filed edges.
Passage of the moss garden.
Slate, schist or black granite laid on a concrete platform.
Paving of the moss garden. Paving of schist fragments.
Rambling rose terrace.
Paving in exotic wood. Pond shores.
Cuttings of black schist.

Patios.

Areas of the museum outside the project.

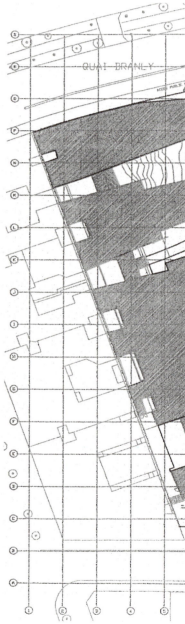

View of the north garden, with the transparent wall along Quai Branly and the wild clematis clearing.

THE DESIGN of the garden does not follow the occidental tradition dominated by the order of symmetrical reason, but offers a soft, undulated space where nature is no longer kept at arm's length, but presented in a scenography of immersion.

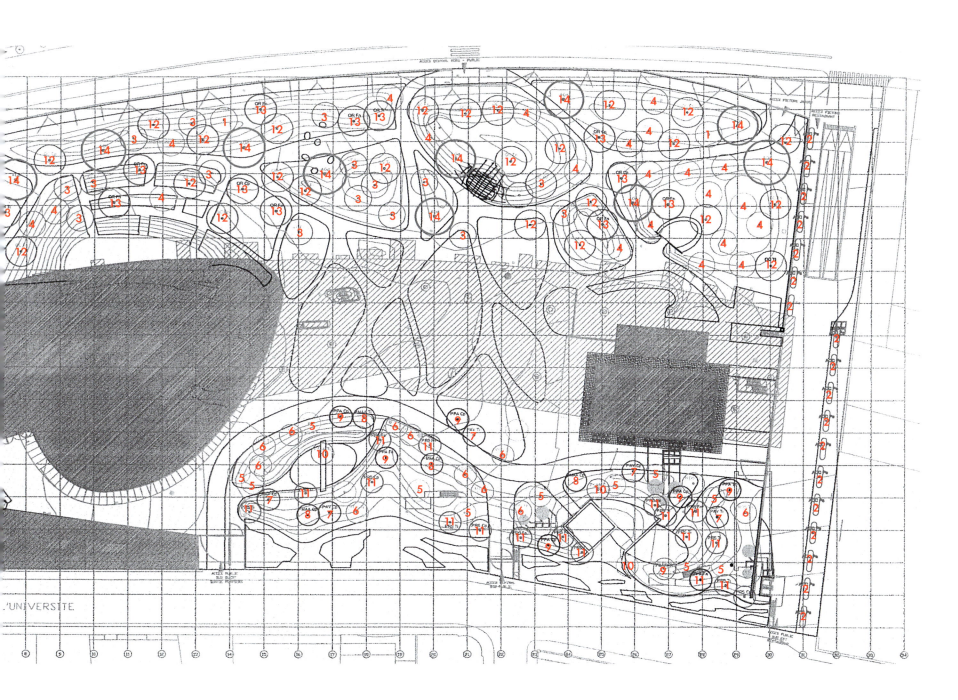

PLAN WITH THE POSITION OF THE TREES

1. *Acer cappadocicum* 2. *Acer campestre* 3. *Acer platanoides*
4. *Acer saccharum* 5. *Magnolia kobus* 6. *Magnolia x soulangeana*
7. *Prunus avium* 8. *Prunus maackii* 9. *Prunus padus* 10. *Prunus sargentii*
11. *Prunus serrula* 12. *Quercus cerris* 13. *Quercus robur*

Abelia grandiflora

Acanthus mollis

Anemone japonica "honorine jobert"

Athyrium filix femina

Carex comans

Carex pendula

Carex plantaginea

Equisetum

Helictotrichon sempervirens

armoured meadow

Hedera helix hibernica (50%), *Hedera helix sagittifolia* (50%)

Heuchera americana "Dale's strain" (35%), *H. brizoiides "virginal"* (35%) *H. cyclindrica* (30%)

Hydrangea paniculata (50%), *H. quercifolia* (50%)

Luzula nivea

Miscanthus sinensis "gracilimus"

Ophiopogon japonicus

Phyllitis scolopendrium

Phyllostachis aurea

Phyllostachis viridistriatus "vagans"

Pleioblastus distichus

Sasa palmata "nebulosa"

Plystichum setiferum

Rosa sinensis "mutabilis"

Scirpus lacustris

Stipa gigantea

Stipa tenuifolia

Taxus baccata

Buxus microphylla

Clematis montana "rubra" and *"tetrarose"*

Rosa filipes Kiftsgate

Rosa longicuspis

Vitis coignetiae

in the bodies of water: *Typhas angustifolia, minima* and *stenophilla*

blocks of basalt covered with sedum and mosses

Views of the humid garden in the southern part.

A carpet of gramineae with blond shadings, a pattern of paths that suggests chance and habit rather than imposition and proportion, absence of direct perspectives and trimmed lawns designed to guide the gaze, the apparent disorder of a light forest, surprises located beyond the rises in the terrain: everything works together to bring out the power of nature.

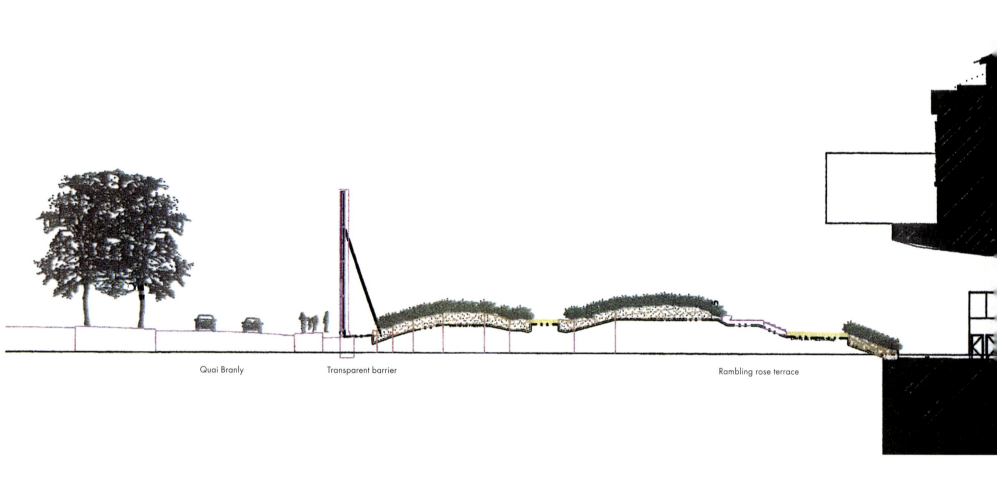

Quai Branly   Transparent barrier   Rambling rose terrace

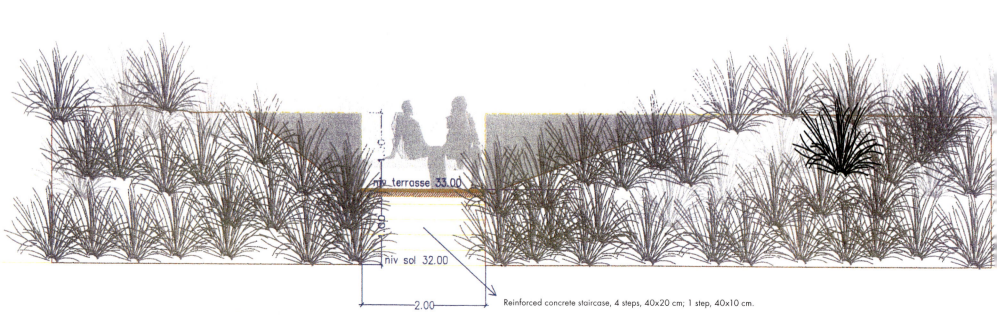

niv terrasse 33.00

niv sol 32.00

2.00   Reinforced concrete staircase, 4 steps, 40x20 cm; 1 step, 40x10 cm.

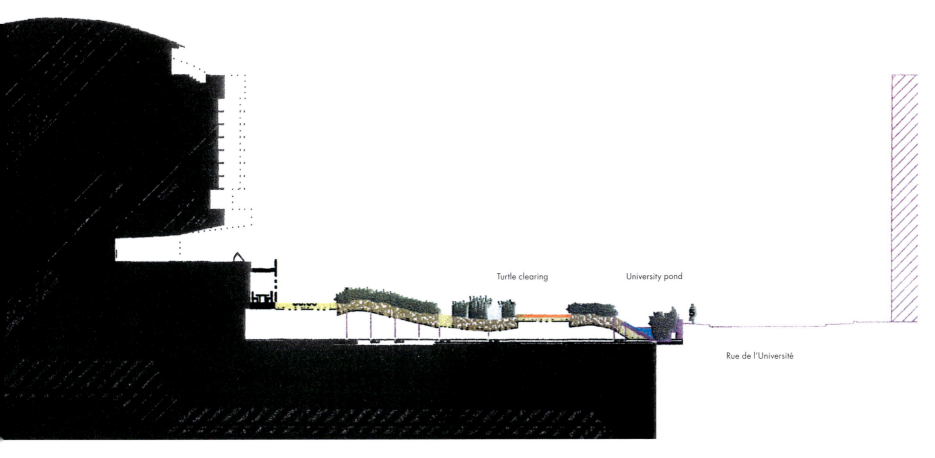

Turtle clearing

University pond

Rue de l'Université

Cross-section, section through the rose terrace *(Rosa filipes Kiftsgate and Rosa longicuspis)*, view of the garden, looking from the interior of the museum toward Quai Branly.

One of the 300 insertions (of insects, plants and seashells) that refer to the animist dictionary.

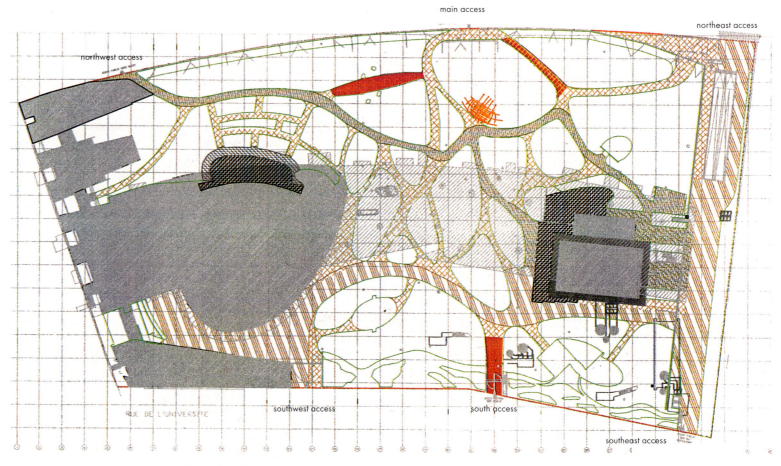

Plan of the paths, section through the Rambling rose terrace and view of the south garden.

northwest access

main access

northeast access

southwest access

south access

southeast access

RUE DE L'UNIVERSITE

vegetable loam

drainage ditch

natural gravel

PATH/ROUTE TYPES

 Heavy traffic, freight and fire brigade

 Occasional heavy traffic

 Pedestrians and possible light vehicles

 Off-project routes

 Parts not accessible to the disabled

To cross the garden it is necessary to walk around the planted islands, while to move from the northern side to the southern side one must pass beneath the building. The network of paths connects the various accessways from Quai Branly, on the northern side, and from Rue de l'Université, to the south, to the museum entrance. The central gate, at the entrance on the Quai Branly riverfront, is an *aling-aling*, a construction typical of Balinese enclosures, in which the frontal curve serves to keep out evil spirits.

East-west longitudinal section, from the eastern border to the Théâtre de verdure, and views of the northern facade of the museum.

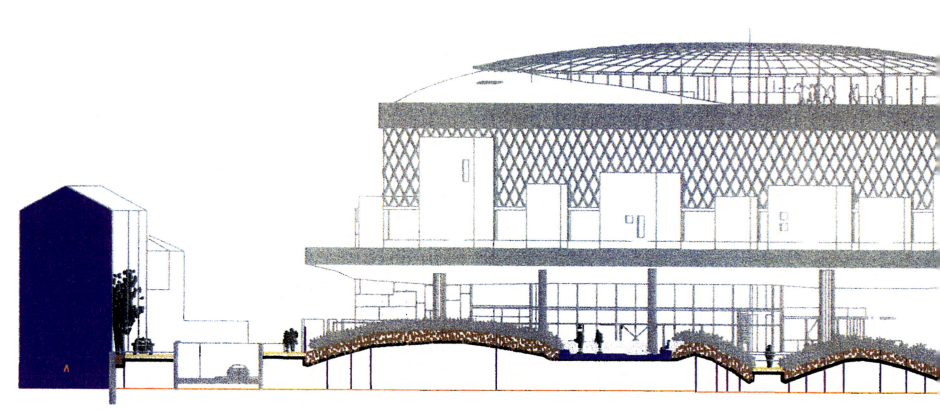

Underground parking ramp

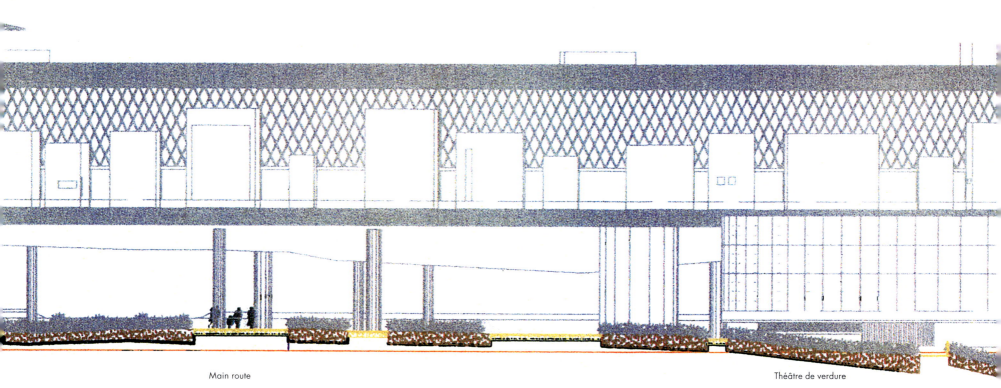

Main route   Théâtre de verdure

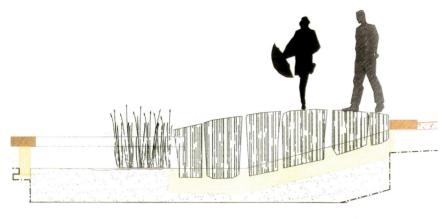

Pond of rushes *(Scirpus lacustris)*.

Turtle bridge composed of monolithic parts in black granite or schist, with hewn or sunburst finish.

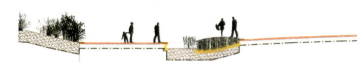

Detail, section and view of the turtle garden and the southern border along Rue de l'Université.

All the forms and objects connected with the clearings evoke the turtle, a legendary animal that has a particular role in the animist and polytheist cosmogonies whose sacred objects are displayed in the museum. The animal is never directly represented; the oval of its shell gives form to the perimeter of the clearings or the profile of a bench, emerges along a path in the guise of rocks covered with moss, or rises as a liana-covered shelter in the middle of the garden.

Detail of the route of access to the museum, on the northern side, and two views of the humid garden, on the southern side, with the pond along Rue de l'Université.

The bridge structure of the museum permits direct connection of the two "tree-lined savannahs". The northern part contains large trees and shrubs, which will grow to reach the level of the roof terrace. To the south, small and medium-sized trees like plum trees and magnolias allow light to enter the windows of the museum. The clearings take form at the intersections of paths, like significant events and pauses.

Views of the Théâtre de verdure and the continuous space below the suspended volume of the museum.

THE ISLAND EURALILLE ABOVE STATION

PARC HENRI MATISSE, LILLE, 1989-1992
Gilles Clément
Agence Empreinte
Associate artist: Claude Courtecuisse
8 hectares

On the previous pages: the parterre with the buildings by Christian de Portzamparc, Claude Vasconi and Jean Nouvel in the background. Selective mowing forms temporary paths suggested by the gardener, simply by cutting the grass: people never venture into the high grass, and the passage across the low grass leads to the formation of a spontaneous path, a so-called "path of desire".

Views of the Derborence island. The walls, shaped in concrete, contain material from the Euralille construction site. In the background, the new residential developments that contributed to finance the creation of the park.

THE PARK has an area of eight hectares and is in direct contact with the TGV station. The epicentre of the project, selected in an international competition, is the Derborence island, an artificial plateau of 3500 square metres with vegetation generated by the planetary *brassage* (mixture), determined by the characteristics of the European boreal biome, along with species from Asia and America. On the top of the island, which is not accessible, after initial planting the vegetation developed spontaneously. To determine the form, the designer chose to reproduce the profile of Antipodes Island, found in New Zealand, precisely at the antipode of Lille; Derborence, on the other hand, is the name of a famous Swiss forest and oasis of untouched nature.

Plan of the park with, at the centre, the irregular profile of the Derborence island and the quad of the parterre (*boulingrin*). To the upper left, the zone of the clearings in the forest, at the border along the railway area.

The island is a miniature highland, raised by seven metres, covering the debris from the Euralille worksite. The earthworks are made with concrete directly poured in the ground, used as formwork; when the earth is removed, a very irregular surface is revealed to which stones, branches and other organic fragments remain attached in a random pattern. The top of the island is not open to visitors, and is entered twice a year by the gardener, who takes note of all the changes and limits his intervention to an indispensable minimum. The island, at the edge of the large grassy parterre (*boulingrin*), is also bordered by an accessible wood that contains four gardens, clearings produced by accidental causes or by the fact that it is impossible for trees to grow in a particular zone.

Eric Lagun, head gardener of the park, during his biannual visit to the top of the Derborence island.

Four clearings appear in the forest.
The Chablis clearing was produced by the natural falling of trees. Willow herbs and digitalis grow amidst intertwined trunks.
The Fire clearing: opening produced by a fire, where pyrophytic species and mosses grow in abundance.
The Marais (marsh) clearing, where only aquatic grasses and flowers grow.
The Lande (moor) clearing, where rocks and dry ground prevent the growth of trees.

View of the Chablis and Lande clearings, with the fallen stones from the ancient walls.

View of the access opening formed by specimens of *Miscanthus sinensis gracillimus*, and of the path that enters the wood, leading to the zone of the clearings.

Section through the park, with the island and the TGV station.
The Roubaix gate, the open central space and an edge organized as a Garden in Movement.

129

THE BOTANICAL CLOISTERS OF THE

ABBEY OF VALLOIRES

GARDENS OF THE ABBEY OF VALLOIRES, 1987-1989
Gilles Clément
Associate landscape designers:
Atelier Acanthe – Philippe Niez, Christophe Ponceau
10 hectares

GARDEN OF EVOLUTION, 2003-2004
Gilles Clément, Miguel Georgieff
Associate landscape designers:
Coloco, Olivier Baert
6000 square metres

Views of the Botanical Cloister, the gardens (drawings by Franck Neau) and the canal with the promenade.

THE PROJECT began through the initiative of a nurseryman, Jean-Louis Cousin, who offered his collection of cold-resistant shrubs from Eastern Europe, Asia and America: a precious heritage, a demonstrative index of the boreal biome. Then the problem was: how to include a range of diverse exotic plants in the design of a garden for public use? Beginning with the need to think of the abbey and the garden as a unified whole, I proposed a central axis starting at the main facade and reaching to the end of the property. The axis terminates in a Botanical Cloister with proportions similar to those of the square cloister of the abbey, a Cistercian settlement reconstructed in 1741. The interval between the yew columns is equal to the span between the pilasters of the peristyle.

Views and plan of the water garden.

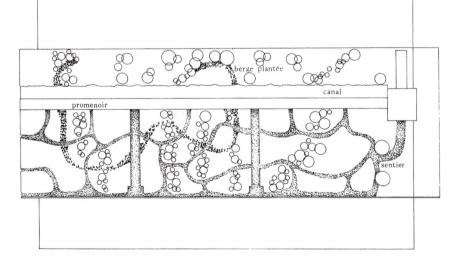

The garden does not have architectural features, but only simple terracing. The very limited budget allowed for no construction: the plants, their layout and rhythm are assigned the role usually played by architecture. During the entire worksite period Philippe Niez supervised the work and the laying of the wooden steps, made with a single ramp without uprights. These light, inexpensive structures were transported by helicopter, leading to significant savings, avoiding the cost of men and machines to work on terrain that was still quite inaccessible.

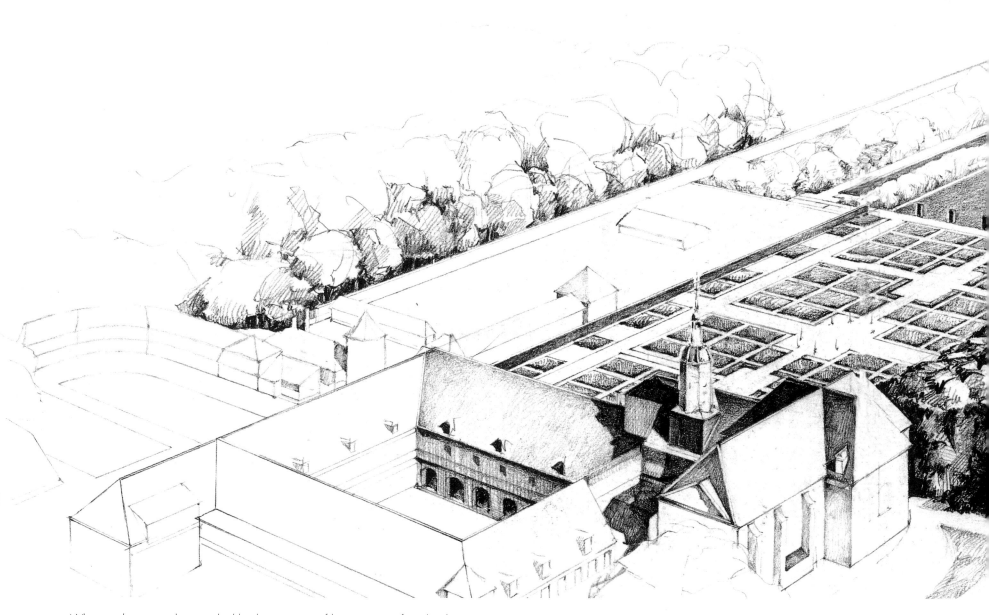

When working in a place marked by the presence of history, one is faced with an inevitable choice: to base the design on ancient presences and residual traces, or to create a completely new image. This project opts for the second hypothesis, but also incorporates significant references to the past. No attempt was made to imitate an image (which in any case did not exist). Instead, the work concentrated on formal schemes that can be considered close to the culture of that era. Therefore the square, the primary figure of Cistercian architecture, is utilized as the geometric matrix of the parterres in front of the western facade, the space of mediation between the abbey and the new gardens.

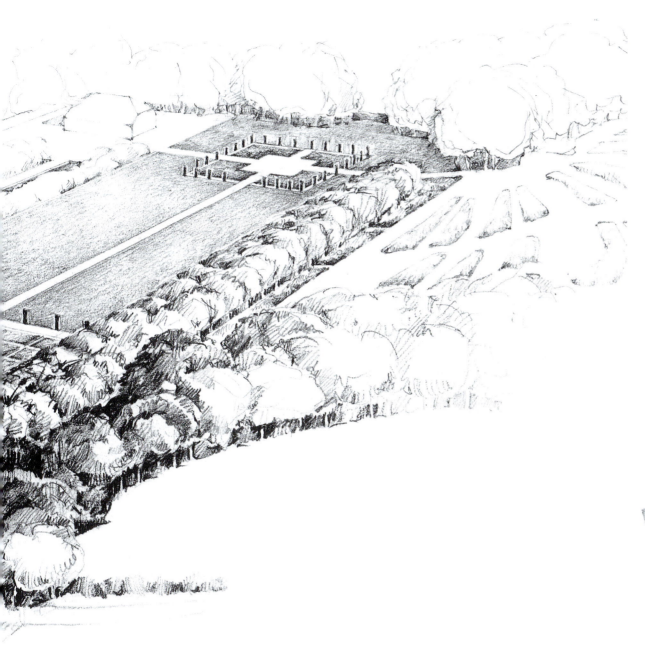

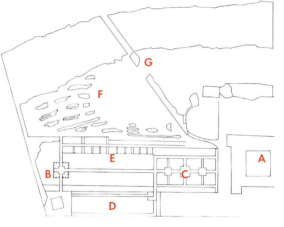

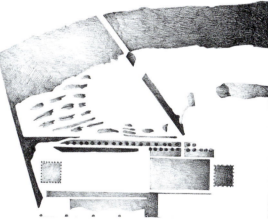

Two working drawings, with the initial idea and its development (drawings by Franck Neau) and, above, the definitive scheme.

Cistercian cloister **A.**
Botanical Cloister **B.**
Rose garden **C.**
Canal and water garden **D.**
White escarpment **E.**
Islands **F.**
Avenues for the game of pall mall (a forerunner of golf) **G.**

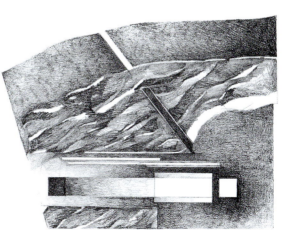

The collection of shrubs in the canal area and on the inclined plane that marks the edge of the parterre.

The shrubs of the collection are arranged on islands that occupy the higher part of the lawn, and around the canal on a lower level. Each island groups different species that are not necessarily similar, but have been chosen for their appearance. The Island of Sweet Thorns contains thorny species, the Island of Winter those in which the bark has spectacular effects at the end of autumn, the Golden Island those with yellow foliage, the Island of Gramineae, and so on. The species that thrive in a humid environment, and those with large leaves, are placed along a new waterway.

A. *Verbascum phlomoides* _ orange mullein

B. *Heracleum mantegazzianum* _ giant hogweed

The medicinal plants

A. *Stachys lanata*

B. *Hosta sieboldiana*

C. *Taxus baccata*

The rose garden

A. *R. rubrifolia*

B. *R. chinensis* 'Mutabilis'

C. *R.* 'Ballerina'

D. *R.* 'Kyushu'

E. *R.* 'Max Graf'

F. *R. filipes* 'Kiftsgate'

G. *R.* 'Yesterday'

H. *R.* 'Nevada'

I. *R.* 'Golden Wings'

J. *R.* 'Wedding Day'

K. *R. nitida*

L. *R. longicuspis*

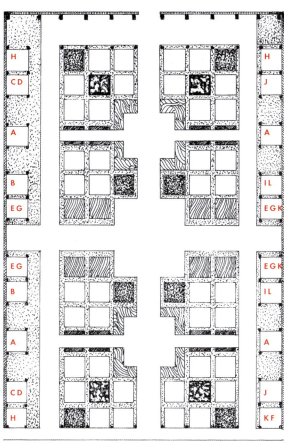

The rose garden, view during the initial phase, and schematic plan.
The roses are mixed with medicinal herbs and vegetables.

Views of the avenue of flowering plum trees.

The lower zone of the garden, with the archaic plants: mosses, ferns, ginkgo, and the first flowering plants: magnolias and buttercups.

THE GARDEN OF EVOLUTION (TRIBUTE TO LAMARCK)

Separated from the gardens of the abbey by a linden avenue, the garden pays tribute to the figure and thought of Jean-Baptiste Lamarck (1744-1829), the naturalist and theorist of evolution born in Picardy, not far from Valloires. I have chosen three key concepts from his teachings:
— Hydrogeology, incessant mechanics sculpting the earth's surface;
— Meteorology, energetic machine that regulates climate and life;
— Biology, approach to the functions of living beings in relation to time, fundamental and revolutionary proposition, basis for the theory of evolution.
In the garden the three concepts appear in the form of Rooms:
— the Room of Erosion (hydrogeology);
— the Room of Living Beings (biology);
— the Room of Clouds (meteorology).
The Rooms are approached by crossing the individual "botanical zones", based on systematic classification. The lower zone contains ancient species, the most archaic flowering plants (magnolias, buttercups) along with primitive species (ferns, mosses). The more evolved species, the more recent arrivals on the path of evolution (umbrellifers, gramineae) are placed in the highest zone, at the end of the route.

The Rooms of Erosion (hydrogeology) and of Clouds (meteorology).

TROPICAL GARDEN AND

FOUNTAIN OF GRASS

FOUNTAIN OF GRASS FOR DRAC, RÉUNION ISLAND, 2003-2004
Gilles Clément, landscape designer
Associate landscape designer: Bruno Duhazé
(Office national des forêts, Réunion)
600 square metres

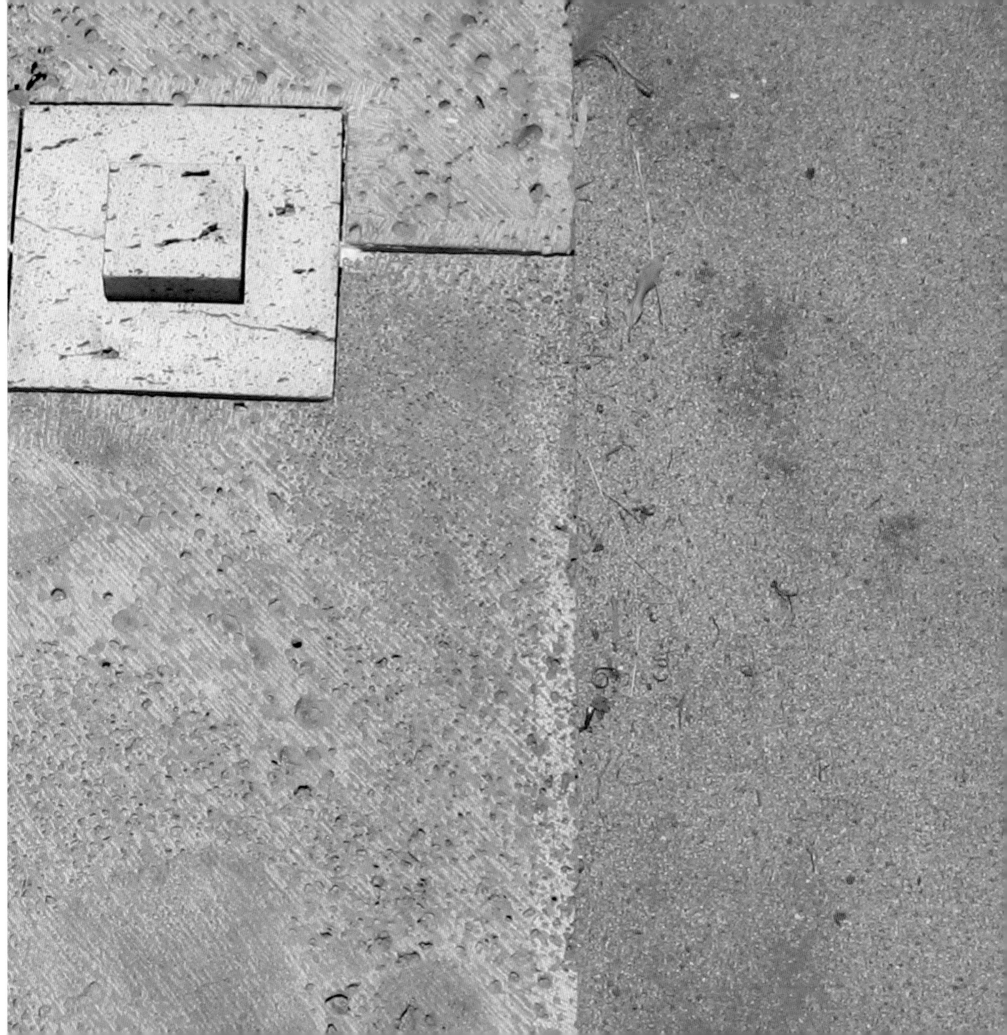

The headquarters of the DRAC (Direction Régionale des Affaires Culturelles, regional directorate of cultural affairs) on Réunion Island, in the Indian Ocean, east of Madagascar, was destroyed by fire in 1999. All that remained were the blackened foundations of a Creole house and the garden, a rectangle open to the street, covered with rubble and charred boughs, and three surviving plants: two palms and one pomegranate tree.

The program for the reconstruction of the garden included major limitations, calling for a parking area for four cars, and a free area to be used for receiving guests. Given the small size of the area, complying with these requests would have meant sacrificing the garden. In the end, after much discussion, the parking area was eliminated, leaving only a vehicle passage for emergencies.

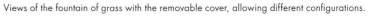
Views of the fountain of grass with the removable cover, allowing different configurations.

Along the edges the garden is defined by other gramineae. *Pennisetum purpureum*, known as napier or elephant grass, is placed along the edge of the building and connects, due to its form and colour, the building and the ground. The foliage wraps the U-shaped basalt blocks that cover the spotlights. On both sides of the house large stands of bamboo conceal the passages that lead to the back, where vetiver and other typical plants of the island grow.

The stabilized soil is composed of sand, clay and calcareous stone. When first installed, its red colour was too intense, but three weeks of constant rain brought out a blonde tone that perfectly adjusted the hue.

The principle is that of a horizontal fountain imagined as a flat sculpture that can be covered with a usable deck to increase the available space for receptions. The idea presented itself as a simple solution capable of reconciling the desire for a garden with the requirements of the programme. This led to the device of the fountain, bristling with pilasters equipped with a groove on which it is possible to attach the removable grating boards. The span between the pilasters measures 80 cm, determined based on the weight of each element, which must be easy for one man to transport, position and remove. For nocturnal lighting a double row of LEDs runs below the border. At first we had imagined a real fountain, but faced with the difficulty of bringing water into the middle of the garden, we decided to replace the water with a plant species, and we chose *Pogonatherum paniceum*, a dwarf bamboo with evergreen leaves.

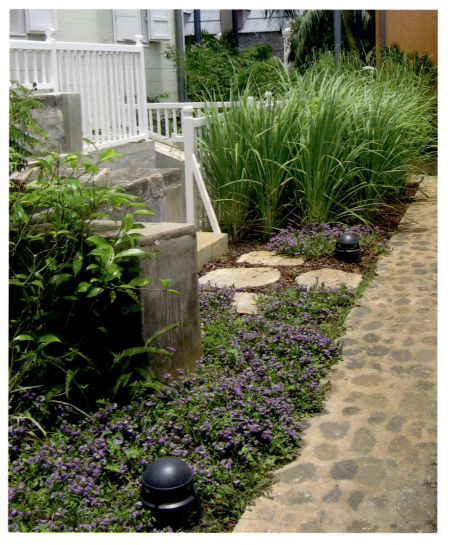

The edges of the garden, the passage leading to the back and the LEDs of the fountain of grass at night.

PARC ANDRÉ CITROËN

PARC ANDRÉ CITROËN, PARIS, 1986-1998
Gilles Clément / Alain Provost, landscape designers
Patrick Berger / J.P. Viguier, J.F. Jodry, architects
Jean-Max Lorca, fountains
Associate landscape designers:
Atelier Acanthe – Philippe Niez,
Christophe Delmar
14 hectares

Aerial view of the park from north to south, with the riverfront in the foreground.

Here are some design principles. Patrick Berger exposes a historical relationship that links the parks on the left bank of the Seine: they are all organized around a main axis that is perpendicular to the river. This approach leads to the form and the monumental scale of the central space, which is now covered with a grass lawn. The rhythm and spirit of the Serial Gardens come from the preliminary drawings of the development to be built at the border, the idea of working the edge with a significant thickness, and the desire to connect the park to the city. The principle of repetition encourages variations. Transmutation, seen as a metaphor of movement, permits utilization and reinterpretation

of the traditional symbols of alchemy. The Serial Gardens, now identified by their colours, also refer to metals, stones, planets, the days of the week. Unlike Rome and other leading cities in urban history, Paris does not have water: public water, for recreation and drinking, and here there is water, accessible, abundant. The Seine borders the park on the western side and therefore the water is everywhere, on the other sides and near the borders, coinciding with the frame that contains the essential part of the gardens: a canal at the foot of the office complex called Ponant, on the southern side; waterways on the ramps that separate the Serial Gardens, to the north; a peristyle of water between the greenhouses, to the east; and a frame of water that isolates the central space from the rest of the park.

With Patrick Berger, we thought about the meaning of building a park in Paris one century after the projects of Alphand, the engineer who under Napoleon III designed many public spaces and gardens, including those of the Champs Elysées, the parks of Monceau and Buttes-Chaumont, and the organization of the two forests on the outskirts of the city, Vincennes and Boulogne. We felt a need to express a manifesto and, with the risk of error regarding the paradigm, to try to write a page of urban history, since we had the possibility to do so. So I wrote an article for the magazine *Urbanisme*, entitled "La friche apprivoisée" (the tamed wasteland), discussing the principles of the Garden in Movement, a text in which I laid out the foundations developed in seven years of experience with my experimental garden at La Vallée. We decided that this new way of looking at nature would form the conceptual basis and the theme of the project. Later, we established a certain number of principles useful for the definition of the overall form of the park and its parts, their organization, the variety and number of the spaces, the possible scales and uses.

View of the esplanade and the parterre, looking toward the Seine.

Eventually, we imagined a progression from natural to artificial, starting at the Seine and proceeding toward the heart of the city. This approach implies freer composition toward the river – the location of the Garden in Movement – and more rigid order on the opposite side. Architecture, as an intermediate term between nature and artifice, organizes and constructs the whole. The combination of the principle of progression and the necessary variation of the Serial Gardens generates the idea of the White Garden and the Black Garden, positioned at the centre of the block as an illustration of artifice. I make this assertion in the awareness of the fact that I am associating the exercise of style based on colours – an English legacy from the garden of the castle of Sissinghurst, an insuperable example – with an exercise on the senses and the need to address, beyond contemporary composition, an urgent theme: that of ecology. This central theme is demonstrated by the Garden in Movement, initially positioned at the centre of the park, whose metaphors and references are found in the immediate surroundings and at the edge of the park: the Garden of Transmutations (the Serial Gardens), the Gardens of Metamorphosis along the canal, the Garden of Wind along the Seine.

Gunnera plants (*Gunnera manicata*) in one of the nymphaea on the canal running along the southern edge.

View of the Serial Gardens from the central parterre, with the inclined plane covered with pink yarrow between the two groves of pruned beech trees.

The front of the southern border, with the rhythmical sequence of nymphaea and fastigiated oaks (shaped in a conical form).

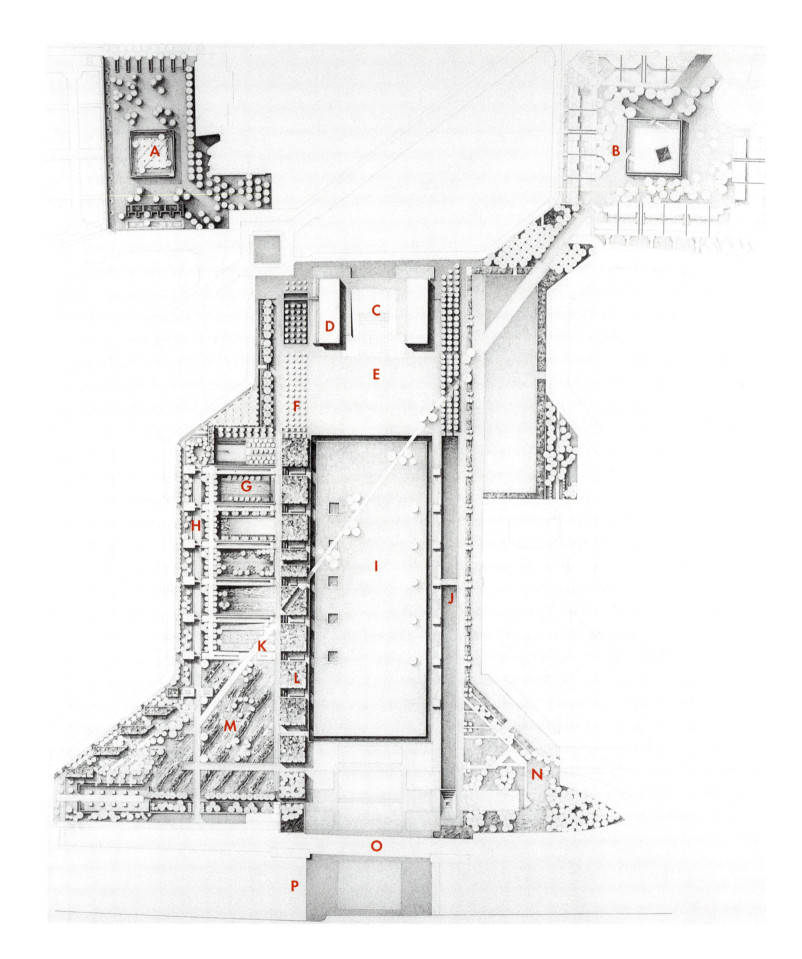

Park plan.

A. White Garden

B. Black Garden

C. Fountain

D. Large greenhouses

E. Esplanade

F. Botanical peristyle

G. Serial Gardens

H. Cold greenhouses

I. Parterre

J. Canal and nymphaea

K. Diagonal path

L. Water border

M. Garden in Movement

N. Rock garden

O. Bridge

P. Riverfront

Views of one of the cold greenhouses and of the border path behind the serial gardens.

In 1970 Citroën decided to close its factories, freeing 22 hectares in the Javel quarter, where the city government of Paris launched a major urban renewal project that also covered the six hectares of the old Grenelle station and the three hectares of the former warehouse of the Hachette publishing house. Since then the developers of the project have built 2500 housing units and commercial spaces organized in eight blocks, many offices, a college, three schools, a daycare centre, a library, a gymnasium, ateliers for artists and a new hospital with 870 beds. Parc André Citroën has an area of 13 hectares and is organized around a large central space, a rectangle of 320 x 130 metres, perpendicular to the Seine. Its overall water surface is one hectare, and there are 25 fountains and eight greenhouses.

The park contains 2500 trees, 70,000 shrubs and 250,000 perennials. Today the overall complex includes a central zone of about 11 hectares and two peripheral gardens, the Leblanc, to the south, with the so-called Black Garden, and the Saint-Charles, containing the White Garden. The central parterre, thanks to the embankment along the riverfront and the bridge of the regional Metro, makes it possible to reach the Seine without obstacles. The parterre of about two hectares is crossed by a diagonal path that begins inside the Black Garden. The long sides of the rectangle are bordered by the Serial Gardens, to the east, and by a 250-metre canal. On the opposite side, with respect to the Seine, a sloping esplanade hosts twin greenhouses, 15 metres high and 45 metres long, that contain an orangery and a Mediterranean and Austral garden. Between the two greenhouses a fountain composed of 120 water jets is directly grafted into the esplanade pavement.

Views of the small valley and the Garden in Movement.

A. *Inula helenium* _ elecampane

B. *Parrotia persica* _ Persian ironwood

C. *Onopordum acanthium* _ Scotch thistle

The Garden in Movement in its first year of life.

Gilles Clément in action with the lawnmower and other views of the Garden in Movement in its second year of existence.

The Garden in Movement is the most popular zone in the park.

A. *Quercus ilex* _ holm oak
B. *Aruncus sylvester* _ goat's beard
C. *Miscanthus sinensis 'Gracillimus'*
D. *Hosta sieboldiana*

The Green Garden: plan and section of the fountain, panoramic view
and partial views of the paths and the fountain.

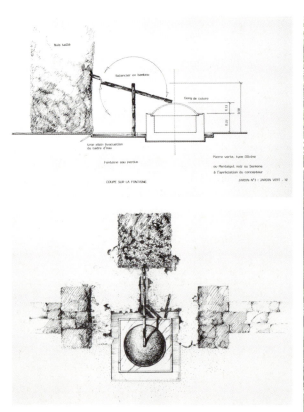

A. *Heracleum mantegazzianum_giant hogweed*
B. *Tellima grandiflora*

A. *Stachys lanata _ lamb's ear*

B. *Tanacetum hybridum*

C. *Mentha piperata*

D. *Delphinum hybridum*

E. *Lavandula "German"*

F. *Geranium endressii*

THE GOLD GARDEN

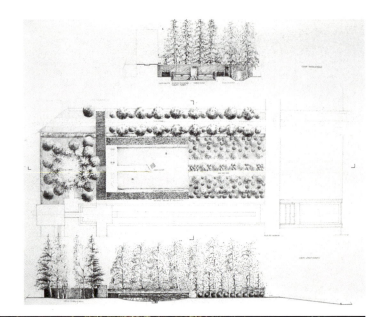

A. *Weigela dorata*

B. *Chamaecerasus nitida aurea*

C. *Lamium galeobdolon* _ yellow archangel

A. *Gleditsia triacanthos "Sunburst"* _ honey locust

B. *Robinia pseudoacacia frisia*

The cascades form an interval between one Serial Garden and the next; the cold greenhouses punctuate the edge and the border path behind the Serial Gardens.

serres froides   jardins sériels   salons d´eau

A. *Pyrus salicifolia*

B. *Festuca glauca*

C. *Euphorbia nicaeensis*

D. *Artemisia absinthium* _ wormwood

E. *Salix purpurea* _ purple willow

F. *Artemisia "Powis Castle"*

THE ORANGE GARDEN

A. *Eremurus bungei*

B. *Kniphofia ibrida*

C. *Agrostis calamagrostis*

Mahaut Clément visiting the Orange Garden.

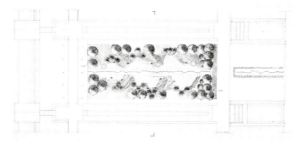

A. *Hieracium aurantiacum*

B. *Eremurus bungei*

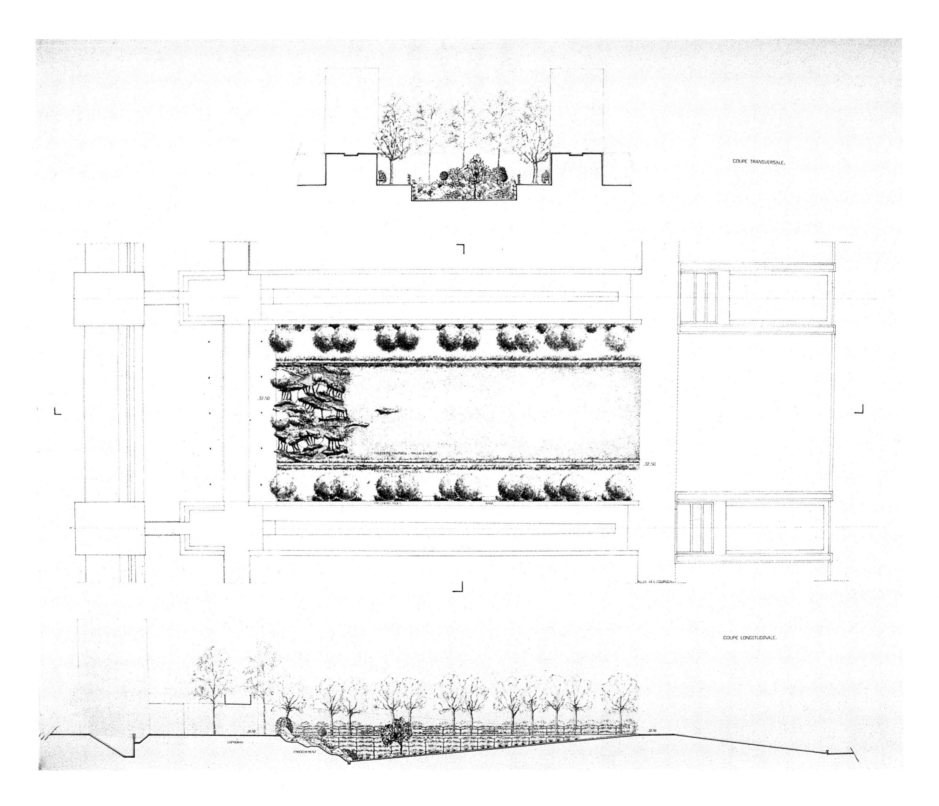

COUPE TRANSVERSALE.

COUPE LONGITUDINALE.

A. *Paronychia kapela serpyllifolia*

B. *Alchemilla mollis*

C. *Lychnis coronaria*

THE EXPERIMENTAL LABORATORY OF LA VALLÉE

THE GARDEN IN MOVEMENT, LA CREUSE, 1977- in progress
Gilles Clément
5 hectares

In 1977 I purchased, in my native region, just 500 metres from the house where I spent vacations as a child, a large valley, sheltered from the winds, where I went to look for beetles and butterflies during my childhood. When I bought it, the land was completely abandoned, and no one had tended it for fourteen years.

I wanted to make a permanent creation, a place of tolerance as a refuge for all living species, an environment in which to live, to live quietly…

As a whole the gardening work at La Vallée consists in constant interpretation of the dynamics at work there. The objective is not to maintain a pre-set image or aesthetic, but to conserve a sculptural and biological balance, open to the greatest possible diversity, to wonder and impermanence.

How to do as much as possible with, as little as possible against? (All my future works would be the result of this philosophy).

How to avoid the noise of the lawnmower, the power saw, the compressor? Is it possible to collaborate with insects, deer and moles?

Laying of tiles and the tent used as a shelter during construction of the house.

There were no constructions on the land, and for two years I became a builder, and constructed a home for myself. Summer came to my aid. We slept in a tent purchased for the occasion.

Maybe we can eliminate weeds simply by making a decision: to eliminate the possibility of judging whether a plant is good or bad.

The Garden in Movement took form as an open hypothesis and it has been enriched, day by day, by new variations linked to the circumstances, the random uncertainties of weather, the mood of the gardener. After four years of observation and the first actions, done in keeping with a new way of doing gardening, I was capable of finding a point of balance between man and nature, and of combining their respective energies for the benefit of biological diversity and, more generally, of life.

Views of the small valley and the house built by Gilles Clément.

The house and the large artificial lake at the bottom of the valley.

Views of the garden

Views of the small valley with the Garden in Movement.

A. *Sambucus nigra* _ black elderberry

B. *Salix cinerea* _ grey willow

C. *Parrotia persica*

D. *Heracleum mantegazzianum* _ giant hogweed

E. *Carpinus betulus* _ hornbeam

One of the most impressive manifestations of the Garden in Movement is the way the species move around on the land. One rapid, spectacular movement is that of the herbaceous species with a short cycle, annuals and biennials (poppies, cornflowers, nigella, digitalis, mullein, reseda) that vanish and reappear, following uneven features of the land…

In the Garden in Movement the paths shift every year, adapting to the spontaneous spread of seeds. Where you could pass yesterday, today the way is blocked, while another passage has opened up in a place that used to be impenetrable. There is continuous modification of circulation spaces and vegetation.
In the photo, a set for the theatre performance of *Les Mamelles de Tirésias*, (the breasts of Tiresias) by Guillaume Apollinaire; direction, sets and costumes by Gilles Clément.

LE CHAMP is a property beside La Vallée, a 7000 square-metre field I use as a laboratory of botanical and entomological diversity. Late annual mowing permits entomological fauna to develop and find shelter, at ground level, before the passage of the machinery. In ten years the botanical evolution shows stabilization of certain perennials (spiked speedwell, malva, soapwort), limited but evident wandering of many biennials (oenotherae, thistles, digitalis, viper's grass), almost complete disappearance of the pioneer annuals present in the initial mixture (phacelia, corn cockles, nigellas, poppies). Many species brought by animals and by the wind appear here and there. In particular, Carthusian pinks, found nowhere in the surroundings for a radius of 50 kilometres, are brought here by birds.

The Rocaille: through La Vallée, beneath a thin layer of fertile soil, there is a rocky, granitic layer. An area of about 100 square metres has been left free of soil and is used as an experimental laboratory to study spontaneous vegetation.

In 2005 I installed a platform in the upper part of Le Champ, 15 square metres of wooden boards to form a deck with a mattress, a portable umbrella and binoculars focused up close, for the observation of plants and animals.

THE AUSTRAL GARDENS AND THE
MEDITERRANEAN INDEX OF RAYOL

MEDITERRANEAN GARDENS OF THE DOMAINE DU RAYOL, VAR,
1989-1994 (evolving project)
Gilles Clément
Associate landscape designers: Philippe Deliau, Albert Tourette
20 hectares

Along the Corniche des Maures, in the stretch between Hyères and Saint-Tropez, the traveller crosses a fragment of brushland that corresponds to the idea of Mediterranean vegetation. Holm oak, cork oak, mastic trees and Aleppo pines, rockrose and filaria, rounded strawberry trees with bright red trunks, tree heather, and on the ground smilax, wild asparagus, serapia, white helleborine, rare orchids and flowers that indicate the acidity of the soil.

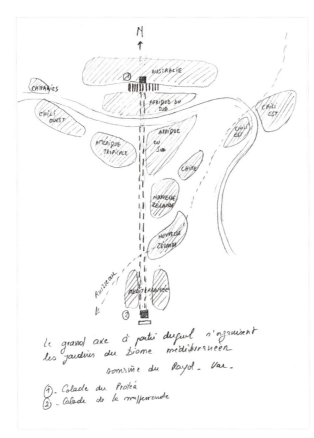

le grand axe à partir duquel s'organisent
les jardins du biome méditerranéen

domaine du Rayol - Var -

① - Calade du Protea
② - Calade de la mappemonde

At the end of the summer of 1988 I proposed the Austral Garden, a title selected to announce a collection of landscapes of the southern hemisphere. The Austral theme arose due to the presence of specimens belonging to that hemisphere, such as eucalyptus and mimosa.

Scattered in southwestern Australia, New Zealand, Tasmania, the Cape of Good Hope and central Chile, the mediterranean sectors belong to traditionally well populated regions, a guarantee of different uses, great biodiversity, specific richness.

In 1990 the arrival in Rayol of a collection of exotic plants, especially cacti, succulents and Mexican yucca, produced two consequences: the introduction of a portion of rocky terrain, which was not planned, and a revision of the concept of the Austral Garden. The term Mediterranean Garden, though apparently less exotic, had the advantage of including California, a source of some remarkable species, certain subtropical sectors of the Americas, well represented at Rayol by venerable specimens of nolina (*beaucarnea*), and also a small part of China, a country in which the mediterranean climate seems to be absent, though it is the place of origin of the chica, of persimmons and albizia. So our biome could grow only as far as the limit set by the plants themselves: whatever would not have been able to grow there "naturally" would not be part of the garden. But we had to allow for some exceptions to this rule: to have flowers one needs water, so an irrigation system was installed. Certain species require soil with good drainage and do not tolerate much clay, so for the South African restio we procured pure quartz sand. The very dry air of the summer could have wilted the New Zealand ferns, so we brought in a bit of fog. How can you resist the temptations of technology?

Drawing and views of the perspective axis, with the
central meadow and the mediterranean rockrose, and
a detail of the sedge field, in the New Zealand garden.

The Art Deco garden of the Rayollet, the callistemon steps and the valley of the ferns, in the New Zealand garden.

The pergola, built in 1910, covered with South African hyacinth, and the villa of the Rayollet.

300 hectares of nature by the sea, between Saint-Tropez and Toulon. In 1988 the Conservatoire du littoral (the public agency for the protection of the French coasts) acquired the property (Domaine) of Rayol, with the aim of making a large public park. The garden is an assemblage of typical species of the mediterranean biome, a planetary index, a combination of singular landscapes, emblems of faraway regions that have a climate similar to that of the Var coast. The garden, therefore, is composed of biologically similar but sculpturally different landscapes, with differences that clarify the relationship between environment and evolution.

For every sector of the mediterranean world and, as a result, for every part of the garden of Rayol, emblematic species exist that are selected, at times, as symbols of their countries of origin, while in certain cases we have identified them as the only species capable of unambiguously suggesting the geographical, ecological or ethnographic themes of the Domaine de Rayol.

The Chilean garden and the Chinese garden.

The Garden in Movement, with the acanthus ground cover, and the fern valley of the New Zealand garden.

Thinning the existing brush, building a flight of steps, tracing a main perspective axis, making some clearings and inserting "landscape gardens", making sure that two of them are never perceived at the same time. The secret, the surprise, must always be protected: apart from the sea, nothing else should ever be visible. Two tasks were necessary to do this: to gain detailed knowledge of the lands, liberated here and there from the destructive force of the locust trees, and to reveal the essence of the exotic landscapes to be installed there.

The Mexican garden, with the cacti and succulents, and the Australian eucalyptus.

Planetary encounters: the Australian blackboys (*Xanthorrhoea preissii*), near Perth, and the fire lily at Sandy Bay, South Africa.

To make the garden I organized trips to New Zealand, California and Australia, in which we discovered the importance of fire in the management of landscapes in the mediterranean world. In Chile, in Australia and above all in South
Africa, we saw many fires, recently burnt areas, or zones coming back to life after fires, with flora that adapts, and a
biological set conditioned by this form of gardening practiced since the dawn of time. This led to the theme of Rayol:
Pyrolandscapes organized in *tableaux vivants*, voyages to the centre of a biological question. How to live with the
cataclysm? Nature responds in a surprising way. The seeds of species tempered by fire reawaken from the slumber of
the thermal shock, while others, like the restio, are activated by the chemical shock produced by substances contained
in smoke. Certain fruits ripen only at high temperatures (hakea, pines), certain trees protect themselves with special
bark (cork oaks, blackboys, passive pyrophytes). Many plants only flower and can only reproduce after a fire (active
pyrophytes). Like the fire lilies of the Cape, the proteas, certain species of the mediterranean brush and *garrigue*, the
Australian mallee, the Chilean *matoral*...

UNDER THE OVERPASS OF THE
GRANDE ARCHE

GARDENS OF THE GRANDE ARCHE, PARIS, LA DÉFENSE, 1991-1998
Gilles Clément/Guillaume Geoffroy-Dechaume, landscape designers
Paul Chemetov, architect
Marc Mimram, engineer
Associate landscape designers: Atelier Acanthe – Pierre Déat
3 hectares

THE GARDENS are located on land disrupted by different highway construction projects that were never completed, leaving a wasteland in their wake. The place lies on the extension of the great monumental axis of Paris, the result of a series of perspective foci that begin at the Louvre and move westward, in keeping with an order typical of the classical garden. The architect Paul Chemetov asked me to participate in the international competition for the extension of the historical axis, and we won the contest by proposing a valley, contradicting the axial principle. With Guillaume Geoffroy-Dechaume, Paul Chemetov and Borja Huidobro we developed a concept of "monuments of fragmentary nature" that was not put into practice. The "jetty" walkway designed by Chemetov and the gardens below the Grande Arche remain, continuing westward for the 600 metres of our intervention. The gardens offer a promenade occupying the narrow strip of land claimed by environmentalists where the A13 highway, suspended in midair, spoiled the sky of Nanterre with its useless architecture. Demolished and rebuilt underground, the highway emerges further on, along the bank of the Seine, where the axis definitively terminates. For that area Guillaume Geoffroy-Dechaume and his team, in my Acanthe atelier, developed a project, the Parc du Chemin de l'Ile, in which I participated only on a conceptual level. The implementation of an initial phase of the project involves the recycling of the waters of the Seine, in an intervention that is effective in terms of both ecology and landscape.

View of the garden, with the Arche in the background, and aerial view before the elimination of the highway; in the background, La Défense, Bois de Boulogne and Paris.

The objective of the project is to counter the hard, windy city with an unpredictable nature that forcefully impresses the visitor, like an inevitable presence. We need to understand that the city with its cement, its frenetic pace, its pollution, does not prevent the arrival of foreign and rare species. The project doesn't respect habits, doesn't use the lists of plants allowed in the city and the rules of alignment, and demonstrates that all species, if they are ecologically compatible with the place and the climate, can find space in the urban environment. Thus the choice of gunnera, a plant with enormous leaves that develops into a rugose surface that can reach two metres in diameter, suspended on a stem of the same size. Arrayed in islands arranged on cobbled paving, the gunneras interrupt the single perspective of La Défense, directed along the promenade and aimed westward. One is forced to walk around them, so one is obliged to encounter them.

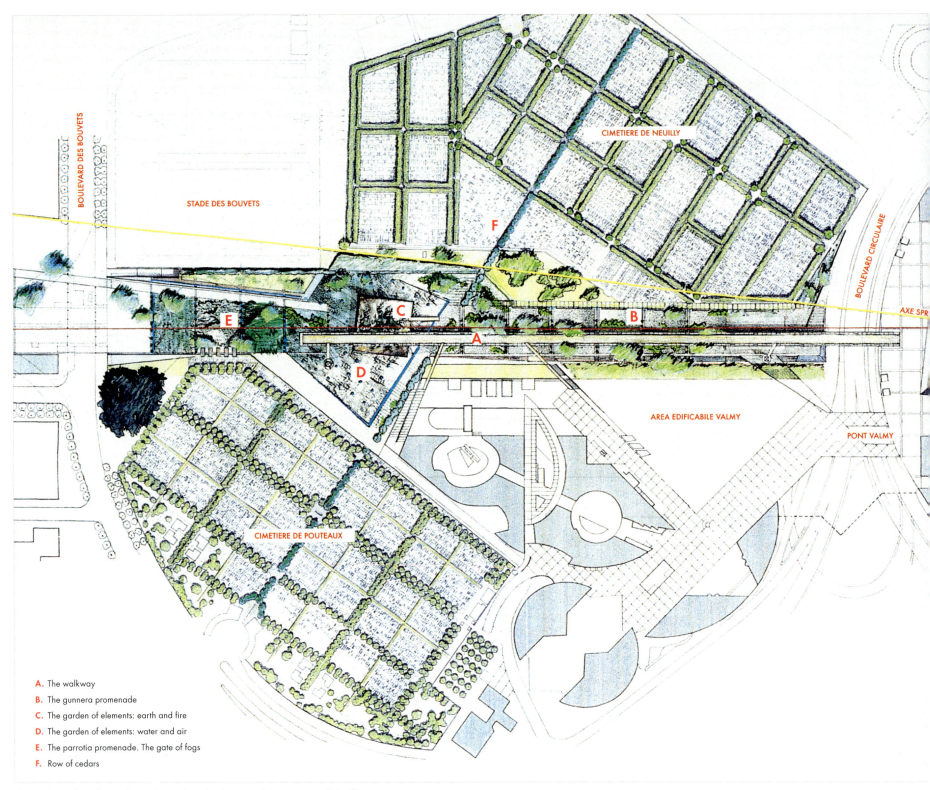

BOULEVARD DES BOUVETS

STADE DES BOUVETS

CIMETIERE DE NEUILLY

BOULEVARD CIRCULAIRE

AXE SPR

F

C

B

E

A

D

AREA EDIFICABILE VALMY

PONT VALMY

CIMETIERE DE POUTEAUX

A. The walkway

B. The gunnera promenade

C. The garden of elements: earth and fire

D. The garden of elements: water and air

E. The parrotia promenade. The gate of fogs

F. Row of cedars

Plan and view from the garden to the north, in the direction of the cemetery of Neuilly.

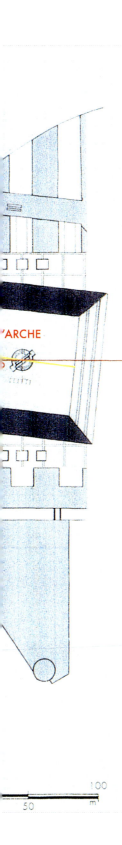

The organization of the cemeteries of Puteaux and Neuilly transforms the series of funerary lots into groves of cherry trees and hornbeams, connected by a diagonal row of cedars. Past the steps of the Grande Arche, looking west along the continuation of the perspective axis, it is possible to see the area of the garden surrounded by dense, almost aggressive vegetation, which in this segment transforms the monumental axis of La Défense into a park.

Scattered planting of large white willows provides the shade required for the species associated with the gunnera (hellebore, holly, periwinkle) and surrounds the walkway.

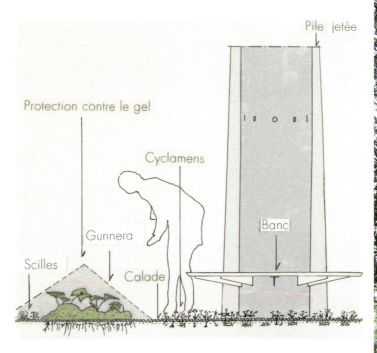

Cross-section. Left to right: squill and gunnera plants, frost protection, cobblestones, cyclamens, bench, walkway pillar.

252

The northern side contains species that flower in the winter, which are used all too rarely in the city: *Stachyurus* with light catkins, *Corylopsis* (winter hazel), *Hamamelis*, winter plum... The southern border overlooks the cemetery of Puteaux. A festoon of gramineae (*Pennisetum sp*) is planted on the bank that runs along the edge of the area, buried beneath a cascade of wisteria and, on the level below, of clematis. The westernmost part of the garden has not yet been built. There is a no-man's land between the gardens of the Grande Arche and the park of the Chemin de l'Île where we hope to see pastures for the animals of the Bonheur farm, which occupies a small leftover parcel at the edge of the axis. If the city can accept the diversity of plants, then why not that of animals? What better demonstration, for the supporters of "peri-urban agriculture", than a cow and some goats, oblivious to the whirlwind of thousands of flying virtual messages buzzing out of the bank headquarters, to turn the whole world upside-down?

Views of the northern border with the balcony of gramineae, and of the southern border, with the hedge and the canal for recycling of rain water.

Miracles, or aberrations, of globalization: the limestone of the paving, very similar to the stone of the Paris basin, comes from Tunisia. Only certain slabs offer a flat, comfortable course. The surfaces covered with cobblestones are held together with mortar that is not damaged by the pressure and deformation caused by the sturdy roots of the willows. Moss forms in the cracks. The birds are invited to the garden, and the little cups cut into certain slabs serve as pools where they can drink.

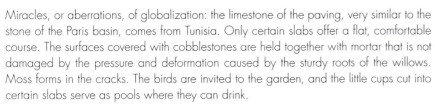

Top row: paving details, with the drinking hollows for birds; bottom row: details of the plating, with the protection baskets for the gunnera plants, in woven bamboo and, on the facing page, boxwood, giant hogweed and gaura.

PUBLICATIONS

Gilles Clément has written extensively: from essays on different subjects to novels. Among his most important publications on the conception and design of landscape are:

Où en est l'herbe? Réflexions sur le jardin planétaire, Actes Sud, 2006.

Gilles Clément. Une écologie humaniste, Aubanel, 2006 (with Louisa Jones).

La sagesse du jardinier, L'oeil neuf éditions, 2004.

Manifeste du tiers paysage, Sujet Objet, 2004.

Éloge des vagabondes, Nil éditions, 2002.

Le jardin planétaire. Réconcilier l'homme et la nature, Albin Michel, 1999, catalogue of the exhibition Le jardin planétaire, Grande Halle de La Villette, Paris, 1999-2000.

Les jardins planétaires, Jean-Michel Place, 1999 (with Guy Tortosa).

Les jardins du Rayol, Actes Sud / Dexia éditions, 1999.

Thomas et le voyageur, Albin Michel, 1997.

Le jardin en mouvement, Sens et Tonka, 1994.

Writings and publications on Gilles Clément:

Lorette Coen, *Gilles Clément: the planetary gardener*, in "'scape" n. 2/2007.

Sonia Lesot (texts), Henri Gaud (photographs), *Les Jardins de Valloires. De la plante à la planète*, Editions Gaud, 2006.

Parc Henri Matisse, Lille, 1996-2000, in "Lotus" n. 122, 2004.

Alessandra Iadicicco, *Gilles Clément e il giardino planetario*, in "Domus" n. 890, 2006.

Alain Roger, *Dal giardino in movimento al giardino planetario*, in "Lotus Navigator" n. 02, 2001.

Marc Bédarida, *Tradizione francese e paradigma ecologico*, in "Lotus" n. 87, 1995.

Les jardins de l'Arche, in "Techniques et architecture" n. 421, 1995.

Une limite du parc Citroën, in "L'architecture d'aujourd'hui" n. 283, 1992.

BIOGRAPHY

Gilles Clément (*1943), *paysagiste* / landscape designer, agronomic engineer, botanist, entomologist, writer, has influenced an entire generation of European landscape designers with his theories and works. He teaches at the ENSP (École Nationale Supérieure du Paysage) of Versailles, and has published many books including *Le jardin en mouvement* (1994), *Le jardin planétaire* (catalogue of the exhibition at La Villette, Paris, 1999), *La sagesse du jardinier* (2004), and two novels, *Thomas et le voyageur* (1997) and *La dernière pierre* (1999). Most of his publications are in French. In Italy his work has been extensively covered by "Domus", "Lotus", "Navigator" and other magazines, and he has published the book *Manifesto del terzo paesaggio* (Quodlibet, 2005). Gilles Clément, Philippe Rahm and Giovanna Borasi are the authors of the bilingual English-French book accompanying the exhibition at the Canadian Center for Architecture CCA in Montreal in 2006/2007, *Environ(ne)ment: Approaches for Tomorrow*. Gilles Clément has created many parks and gardens, including the highly acclaimed Parc André Citroën and the park of Quai Branly Museum in Paris, the gardens of the Grande Arche at La Défense, and Parc Henri Matisse in Lille, as well as projects in the historic parks of Blois and Valloires. Through the concept of the "third landscape" he has shown how biodiversity establishes itself in unpredictable places (metropolitan centres, at the margins of large and small infrastructures, in abandoned areas), while around the slogan of the "garden in movement" he has organized a series of minimal strategies for creating gardens "together with" nature instead of "against" it. The third guiding concept is that of the "planetary garden", illustrated in an exhibition held at the Grande Halle de la Villette (1999), a vision of the entire planet as a single ecological environment, an interdependent system in which we are all active and passive guests, and where all our gestures have repercussions on the harmony (or dissonance) of the whole. Based on a reworking of ecological and biological themes and on the invention of an original design approach, the work of Clément represents an essential contribution, today, to the development of a new, more appropriate way of thinking about our relationship with the environment in which we live.

ACKNOWLEDGEMENTS

The book is the result of the courtesy and cooperation of Gilles Clément, who believed in our project and supported and aided it without reserve. So the first thank you is for him, both the subject of this book and the creator of the gardens it documents. Nearly all the images that appear in the book are his as well, coming directly from his archives. The exceptions to this rule are the photographs (on pages 102, 105, 109, 110, 113, 208-09, 212-13, 214, 222-23, 248) taken by Francesca Tatarella during visits to the gardens and to La Vallée. Francesca Tatarella also worked on the organization of the project and on the translation of the original Italian edition, together with Daniela Re, of the interview, which was recorded in the private garden of La Vallée (Creuse, France) on 21 April 2007. The texts gathered under the heading *Guidelines for the Planetary Garden* have been selected from books included in the bibliography, while the texts explaining the individual projects are free reports of the descriptions supplied by GC.

Among the many people who provided me with knowledge, stimuli for reflection and ideas that, in many different ways, have found their way into this book, I would like to thank Franco Purini, who many years ago taught me a great deal about the relationship between architecture and landscape; Pierluigi Nicolin, the first to publish an important critical contribution on the work of GC in Italy, I believe, in the magazine "Navigator"; and Raffaello Cecchi, with whom I have enjoyed many discussions (and some projects) on architecture, landscape and gardens. I would also like to thank Carolina Fois, who got me involved in her experience at the ENSP (École Nationale Supérieure du Paysage) of Versailles, permitting me to become better acquainted with GC, in his work as a landscape designer and teacher. An important contribution was also made by Attilio Gobbi, who encouraged a shared professional project in Italy, together with GC, offering me an unexpected opportunity for closer knowledge and effective direct participation.

Thanks are also due, for various aspects, to my companions and colleagues in my experiences in publishing and university work: Lorenzo Gaetani, with whom I shared the first in-depth studies on landscape; Giovanni Corbellini, who helped me to reflect the role of the architecture critic; Marco Navarra, an architect disturbed by the demon of landscape; Rita Capezzuto, a perceptive observer of the European scene; and Matteo Codignola, a generous, supportive source of very useful indications on publications. I also want to extend my thanks and best wishes to Marco Tatarella, who has assumed responsibility for the national and international fate of this volume.

Finally, heartfelt thanks to all those whose moral support and concrete assistance have permitted me to dedicate this book: to my parents, my companion Alessandra and my two magnificent sons, Filippo and Giacomo.

Alessandro Rocca